North Carolina
Grade 5
Science

Dear Future Exam Success Story

First of all, **THANK YOU** for purchasing Mometrix study materials!

Second, congratulations! You are one of the few determined test-takers who are committed to doing whatever it takes to excel on your exam. **You have come to the right place.** We developed these study materials with one goal in mind: to deliver you the information you need in a format that's concise and easy to use.

In addition to optimizing your guide for the content of the test, we've outlined our recommended steps for breaking down the preparation process into small, attainable goals so you can make sure you stay on track.

We've also analyzed the entire test-taking process, identifying the most common pitfalls and showing how you can overcome them and be ready for any curveball the test throws you.

Standardized testing is one of the biggest obstacles on your road to success, which only increases the importance of doing well in the high-pressure, high-stakes environment of test day. Your results on this test could have a significant impact on your future, and this guide provides the information and practical advice to help you achieve your full potential on test day.

Your success is our success

We would love to hear from you! If you would like to share the story of your exam success or if you have any questions or comments in regard to our products, please contact us at **800-673-8175** or **support@mometrix.com**.

Thanks again for your business and we wish you continued success!

Sincerely,
The Mometrix Test Preparation Team

Written and edited by the Mometrix Test Preparation Team
Printed in the United States of America

Table of Contents

Introduction

Thank you for purchasing this resource! You have made the choice to prepare yourself for a test that could have a huge impact on your future, and this guide is designed to help you be fully ready for test day. Obviously, it's important to have a solid understanding of the test material, but you also need to be prepared for the unique environment and stressors of the test, so that you can perform to the best of your abilities.

For this purpose, the first section that appears in this guide is the **Success Strategies**. We've devoted countless hours to meticulously researching what works and what doesn't, and we've boiled down our findings to the most impactful steps you can take to improve your performance on the test. We start at the beginning with study planning and move through the preparation process, all the way to the testing strategies that will help you get the most out of what you know when you're finally sitting in front of the test.

We recommend that you start preparing for your test as far in advance as possible. However, if you've bought this guide as a last-minute study resource and only have a few days before your test, we recommend that you skip over the first two Success Strategies since they address a long-term study plan.

If you struggle with **test anxiety**, we strongly encourage you to check out our recommendations for how you can overcome it. Test anxiety is a formidable foe, but it can be beaten, and we want to make sure you have the tools you need to defeat it.

Strategy #1 – Plan Big, Study Small

There's a lot riding on your performance. If you want to ace this test, you're going to need to keep your skills sharp and the material fresh in your mind. You need a plan that lets you review everything you need to know while still fitting in your schedule. We'll break this strategy down into three categories.

Information Organization

Start with the information you already have: the official test outline. From this, you can make a complete list of all the concepts you need to cover before the test. Organize these concepts into groups that can be studied together, and create a list of any related vocabulary you need to learn so you can brush up on any difficult terms. You'll want to keep this vocabulary list handy once you actually start studying since you may need to add to it along the way.

Time Management

Once you have your set of study concepts, decide how to spread them out over the time you have left before the test. Break your study plan into small, clear goals so you have a manageable task for each day and know exactly what you're doing. Then just focus on one small step at a time. When you manage your time this way, you don't need to spend hours at a time studying. Studying a small block of content for a short period each day helps you retain information better and avoid stressing over how much you have left to do. You can relax knowing that you have a plan to cover everything in time. In order for this strategy to be effective though, you have to start studying early and stick to your schedule. Avoid the exhaustion and futility that comes from last-minute cramming!

Study Environment

The environment you study in has a big impact on your learning. Studying in a coffee shop, while probably more enjoyable, is not likely to be as fruitful as studying in a quiet room. It's important to keep distractions to a minimum. You're only planning to study for a short block of time, so make the most of it. Don't pause to check your phone or get up to find a snack. It's also important to **avoid multitasking**. Research has consistently shown that multitasking will make your studying dramatically less effective. Your study area should also be comfortable and well-lit so you don't have the distraction of straining your eyes or sitting on an uncomfortable chair.

The time of day you study is also important. You want to be rested and alert. Don't wait until just before bedtime. Study when you'll be most likely to comprehend and remember. Even better, if you know what time of day your test will be, set that time aside for study. That way your brain will be used to working on that subject at that specific time and you'll have a better chance of recalling information.

Finally, it can be helpful to team up with others who are studying for the same test. Your actual studying should be done in as isolated an environment as possible, but the work of organizing the information and setting up the study plan can be divided up. In between study sessions, you can discuss with your teammates the concepts that you're all studying and quiz each other on the details. Just be sure that your teammates are as serious about the test as you are. If you find that your study time is being replaced with social time, you might need to find a new team.

Strategy #2 – Make Your Studying Count

You're devoting a lot of time and effort to preparing for this test, so you want to be absolutely certain it will pay off. This means doing more than just reading the content and hoping you can remember it on test day. It's important to make every minute of study count. There are two main areas you can focus on to make your studying count.

Retention

It doesn't matter how much time you study if you can't remember the material. You need to make sure you are retaining the concepts. To check your retention of the information you're learning, try recalling it at later times with minimal prompting. Try carrying around flashcards and glance at one or two from time to time or ask a friend who's also studying for the test to quiz you.

To enhance your retention, look for ways to put the information into practice so that you can apply it rather than simply recalling it. If you're using the information in practical ways, it will be much easier to remember. Similarly, it helps to solidify a concept in your mind if you're not only reading it to yourself but also explaining it to someone else. Ask a friend to let you teach them about a concept you're a little shaky on (or speak aloud to an imaginary audience if necessary). As you try to summarize, define, give examples, and answer your friend's questions, you'll understand the concepts better and they will stay with you longer. Finally, step back for a big picture view and ask yourself how each piece of information fits with the whole subject. When you link the different concepts together and see them working together as a whole, it's easier to remember the individual components.

Finally, practice showing your work on any multi-step problems, even if you're just studying. Writing out each step you take to solve a problem will help solidify the process in your mind, and you'll be more likely to remember it during the test.

Modality

Modality simply refers to the means or method by which you study. Choosing a study modality that fits your own individual learning style is crucial. No two people learn best in exactly the same way, so it's important to know your strengths and use them to your advantage.

For example, if you learn best by visualization, focus on visualizing a concept in your mind and draw an image or a diagram. Try color-coding your notes, illustrating them, or creating symbols that will trigger your mind to recall a learned concept. If you learn best by hearing or discussing information, find a study partner who learns the same way or read aloud to yourself. Think about how to put the information in your own words. Imagine that you are giving a lecture on the topic and record yourself so you can listen to it later.

For any learning style, flashcards can be helpful. Organize the information so you can take advantage of spare moments to review. Underline key words or phrases. Use different colors for different categories. Mnemonic devices (such as creating a short list in which every item starts with the same letter) can also help with retention. Find what works best for you and use it to store the information in your mind most effectively and easily.

Strategy #3 – Practice the Right Way

Your success on test day depends not only on how many hours you put into preparing, but also on whether you prepared the right way. It's good to check along the way to see if your studying is paying off. One of the most effective ways to do this is by taking practice tests to evaluate your progress. Practice tests are useful because they show exactly where you need to improve. Every time you take a practice test, pay special attention to these three groups of questions:

- The questions you got wrong
- The questions you had to guess on, even if you guessed right
- The questions you found difficult or slow to work through

This will show you exactly what your weak areas are, and where you need to devote more study time. Ask yourself why each of these questions gave you trouble. Was it because you didn't understand the material? Was it because you didn't remember the vocabulary? Do you need more repetitions on this type of question to build speed and confidence? Dig into those questions and figure out how you can strengthen your weak areas as you go back to review the material.

Additionally, many practice tests have a section explaining the answer choices. It can be tempting to read the explanation and think that you now have a good understanding of the concept. However, an explanation likely only covers part of the question's broader context. Even if the explanation makes perfect sense, **go back and investigate** every concept related to the question until you're positive you have a thorough understanding.

As you go along, keep in mind that the practice test is just that: practice. Memorizing these questions and answers will not be very helpful on the actual test because it is unlikely to have any of the same exact questions. If you only know the right answers to the sample questions, you won't be prepared for the real thing. **Study the concepts** until you understand them fully, and then you'll be able to answer any question that shows up on the test.

It's important to wait on the practice tests until you're ready. If you take a test on your first day of study, you may be overwhelmed by the amount of material covered and how much you need to learn. Work up to it gradually.

On test day, you'll need to be prepared for answering questions, managing your time, and using the test-taking strategies you've learned. It's a lot to balance, like a mental marathon that will have a big impact on your future. Like training for a marathon, you'll need to start slowly and work your way up. When test day arrives, you'll be ready.

Start with the strategies you've read in the first two Success Strategies—plan your course and study in the way that works best for you. If you have time, consider using multiple study resources to get different approaches to the same concepts. It can be helpful to see difficult concepts from more than one angle. Then find a good source for practice tests. Many times, the test website will suggest potential study resources or provide sample tests.

Practice Test Strategy

If you're able to find at least three practice tests, we recommend this strategy:

UNTIMED AND OPEN-BOOK PRACTICE

Take the first test with no time constraints and with your notes and study guide handy. Take your time and focus on applying the strategies you've learned.

TIMED AND OPEN-BOOK PRACTICE

Take the second practice test open-book as well, but set a timer and practice pacing yourself to finish in time.

TIMED AND CLOSED-BOOK PRACTICE

Take any other practice tests as if it were test day. Set a timer and put away your study materials. Sit at a table or desk in a quiet room, imagine yourself at the testing center, and answer questions as quickly and accurately as possible.

Keep repeating timed and closed-book tests on a regular basis until you run out of practice tests or it's time for the actual test. Your mind will be ready for the schedule and stress of test day, and you'll be able to focus on recalling the material you've learned.

Strategy #4 – Pace Yourself

Once you're fully prepared for the material on the test, your biggest challenge on test day will be managing your time. Just knowing that the clock is ticking can make you panic even if you have plenty of time left. Work on pacing yourself so you can build confidence against the time constraints of the exam. Pacing is a difficult skill to master, especially in a high-pressure environment, so **practice is vital**.

Set time expectations for your pace based on how much time is available. For example, if a section has 60 questions and the time limit is 30 minutes, you know you have to average 30 seconds or less per question in order to answer them all. Although 30 seconds is the hard limit, set 25 seconds per question as your goal, so you reserve extra time to spend on harder questions. When you budget extra time for the harder questions, you no longer have any reason to stress when those questions take longer to answer.

Don't let this time expectation distract you from working through the test at a calm, steady pace, but keep it in mind so you don't spend too much time on any one question. Recognize that taking extra time on one question you don't understand may keep you from answering two that you do understand later in the test. If your time limit for a question is up and you're still not sure of the answer, mark it and move on, and come back to it later if the time and the test format allow. If the testing format doesn't allow you to return to earlier questions, just make an educated guess; then put it out of your mind and move on.

On the easier questions, be careful not to rush. It may seem wise to hurry through them so you have more time for the challenging ones, but it's not worth missing one if you know the concept and just didn't take the time to read the question fully. Work efficiently but make sure you understand the question and have looked at all of the answer choices, since more than one may seem right at first.

Even if you're paying attention to the time, you may find yourself a little behind at some point. You should speed up to get back on track, but do so wisely. Don't panic; just take a few seconds less on each question until you're caught up. Don't guess without thinking, but do look through the answer choices and eliminate any you know are wrong. If you can get down to two choices, it is often worthwhile to guess from those. Once you've chosen an answer, move on and don't dwell on any that you skipped or had to hurry through. If a question was taking too long, chances are it was one of the harder ones, so you weren't as likely to get it right anyway.

On the other hand, if you find yourself getting ahead of schedule, it may be beneficial to slow down a little. The more quickly you work, the more likely you are to make a careless mistake that will affect your score. You've budgeted time for each question, so don't be afraid to spend that time. Practice an efficient but careful pace to get the most out of the time you have.

Test-Taking Strategies

This section contains a list of test-taking strategies that you may find helpful as you work through the test. By taking what you know and applying logical thought, you can maximize your chances of answering any question correctly!

It is very important to realize that every question is different and every person is different: no single strategy will work on every question, and no single strategy will work for every person. That's why we've included all of them here, so you can try them out and determine which ones work best for different types of questions and which ones work best for you.

Question Strategies

✓ Read Carefully

Read the question and the answer choices carefully. Don't miss the question because you misread the terms. You have plenty of time to read each question thoroughly and make sure you understand what is being asked. Yet a happy medium must be attained, so don't waste too much time. You must read carefully and efficiently.

✓ Contextual Clues

Look for contextual clues. If the question includes a word you are not familiar with, look at the immediate context for some indication of what the word might mean. Contextual clues can often give you all the information you need to decipher the meaning of an unfamiliar word. Even if you can't determine the meaning, you may be able to narrow down the possibilities enough to make a solid guess at the answer to the question.

✓ Prefixes

If you're having trouble with a word in the question or answer choices, try dissecting it. Take advantage of every clue that the word might include. Prefixes can be a huge help. Usually, they allow you to determine a basic meaning. *Pre-* means before, *post-* means after, *pro-* is positive, *de-* is negative. From prefixes, you can get an idea of the general meaning of the word and try to put it into context.

✓ Hedge Words

Watch out for critical hedge words, such as *likely, may, can, often, almost, mostly, usually, generally, rarely,* and *sometimes*. Question writers insert these hedge phrases to cover every possibility. Often an answer choice will be wrong simply because it leaves no room for exception. Be on guard for answer choices that have definitive words such as *exactly* and *always*.

✓ Switchback Words

Stay alert for *switchbacks*. These are the words and phrases frequently used to alert you to shifts in thought. The most common switchback words are *but, although*, and *however*. Others include *nevertheless, on the other hand, even though, while, in spite of, despite*, and *regardless of*. Switchback words are important to catch because they can change the direction of the question or an answer choice.

✓ FACE VALUE

When in doubt, use common sense. Accept the situation in the problem at face value. Don't read too much into it. These problems will not require you to make wild assumptions. If you have to go beyond creativity and warp time or space in order to have an answer choice fit the question, then you should move on and consider the other answer choices. These are normal problems rooted in reality. The applicable relationship or explanation may not be readily apparent, but it is there for you to figure out. Use your common sense to interpret anything that isn't clear.

Answer Choice Strategies

✓ ANSWER SELECTION

The most thorough way to pick an answer choice is to identify and eliminate wrong answers until only one is left, then confirm it is the correct answer. Sometimes an answer choice may immediately seem right, but be careful. The test writers will usually put more than one reasonable answer choice on each question, so take a second to read all of them and make sure that the other choices are not equally obvious. As long as you have time left, it is better to read every answer choice than to pick the first one that looks right without checking the others.

✓ ANSWER CHOICE FAMILIES

An answer choice family consists of two (in rare cases, three) answer choices that are very similar in construction and cannot all be true at the same time. If you see two answer choices that are direct opposites or parallels, one of them is usually the correct answer. For instance, if one answer choice says that quantity *x* increases and another either says that quantity *x* decreases (opposite) or says that quantity *y* increases (parallel), then those answer choices would fall into the same family. An answer choice that doesn't match the construction of the answer choice family is more likely to be incorrect. Most questions will not have answer choice families, but when they do appear, you should be prepared to recognize them.

✓ ELIMINATE ANSWERS

Eliminate answer choices as soon as you realize they are wrong, but make sure you consider all possibilities. If you are eliminating answer choices and realize that the last one you are left with is also wrong, don't panic. Start over and consider each choice again. There may be something you missed the first time that you will realize on the second pass.

✓ AVOID FACT TRAPS

Don't be distracted by an answer choice that is factually true but doesn't answer the question. You are looking for the choice that answers the question. Stay focused on what the question is asking for so you don't accidentally pick an answer that is true but incorrect. Always go back to the question and make sure the answer choice you've selected actually answers the question and is not merely a true statement.

✓ EXTREME STATEMENTS

In general, you should avoid answers that put forth extreme actions as standard practice or proclaim controversial ideas as established fact. An answer choice that states the "process should be used in certain situations, if..." is much more likely to be correct than one that states the "process should be discontinued completely." The first is a calm rational statement and doesn't even make a definitive, uncompromising stance, using a hedge word *if* to provide wiggle room, whereas the second choice is far more extreme.

⊘ Benchmark

As you read through the answer choices and you come across one that seems to answer the question well, mentally select that answer choice. This is not your final answer, but it's the one that will help you evaluate the other answer choices. The one that you selected is your benchmark or standard for judging each of the other answer choices. Every other answer choice must be compared to your benchmark. That choice is correct until proven otherwise by another answer choice beating it. If you find a better answer, then that one becomes your new benchmark. Once you've decided that no other choice answers the question as well as your benchmark, you have your final answer.

⊘ Predict the Answer

Before you even start looking at the answer choices, it is often best to try to predict the answer. When you come up with the answer on your own, it is easier to avoid distractions and traps because you will know exactly what to look for. The right answer choice is unlikely to be word-for-word what you came up with, but it should be a close match. Even if you are confident that you have the right answer, you should still take the time to read each option before moving on.

General Strategies

⊘ Tough Questions

If you are stumped on a problem or it appears too hard or too difficult, don't waste time. Move on! Remember though, if you can quickly check for obviously incorrect answer choices, your chances of guessing correctly are greatly improved. Before you completely give up, at least try to knock out a couple of possible answers. Eliminate what you can and then guess at the remaining answer choices before moving on.

⊘ Check Your Work

Since you will probably not know every term listed and the answer to every question, it is important that you get credit for the ones that you do know. Don't miss any questions through careless mistakes. If at all possible, try to take a second to look back over your answer selection and make sure you've selected the correct answer choice and haven't made a costly careless mistake (such as marking an answer choice that you didn't mean to mark). This quick double check should more than pay for itself in caught mistakes for the time it costs.

⊘ Pace Yourself

It's easy to be overwhelmed when you're looking at a page full of questions; your mind is confused and full of random thoughts, and the clock is ticking down faster than you would like. Calm down and maintain the pace that you have set for yourself. Especially as you get down to the last few minutes of the test, don't let the small numbers on the clock make you panic. As long as you are on track by monitoring your pace, you are guaranteed to have time for each question.

⊘ Don't Rush

It is very easy to make errors when you are in a hurry. Maintaining a fast pace in answering questions is pointless if it makes you miss questions that you would have gotten right otherwise. Test writers like to include distracting information and wrong answers that seem right. Taking a little extra time to avoid careless mistakes can make all the difference in your test score. Find a pace that allows you to be confident in the answers that you select.

✅ Keep Moving

Panicking will not help you pass the test, so do your best to stay calm and keep moving. Taking deep breaths and going through the answer elimination steps you practiced can help to break through a stress barrier and keep your pace.

Final Notes

The combination of a solid foundation of content knowledge and the confidence that comes from practicing your plan for applying that knowledge is the key to maximizing your performance on test day. As your foundation of content knowledge is built up and strengthened, you'll find that the strategies included in this chapter become more and more effective in helping you quickly sift through the distractions and traps of the test to isolate the correct answer.

Now that you're preparing to move forward into the test content chapters of this book, be sure to keep your goal in mind. As you read, think about how you will be able to apply this information on the test. If you've already seen sample questions for the test and you have an idea of the question format and style, try to come up with questions of your own that you can answer based on what you're reading. This will give you valuable practice applying your knowledge in the same ways you can expect to on test day.

Good luck and good studying!

Physical Science

Matter and its Interactions

Properties of Matter

Matter is anything that takes up space and has weight. Even air has weight and takes up space. All types of matter have different properties that can be observed or measured. There are many properties of matter, including temperature, mass, magnetism, and the ability to sink or float.

Intensive and Extensive Physical Properties of Matter

Intensive properties are properties that do not change when the size of a material changes. Density, melting point, freezing point, boiling point, color, chemical reactivity, luster, malleability, and electrical conductivity are examples of intensive properties. In contrast, **extensive properties** do change when the size of a material changes. Volume, mass, and weight are examples of extensive properties. Some intensive properties can be known just by looking at an object, such as color and state of matter. Other intensive and extensive properties can only be measured using special tools or by using tests to learn more about an object. Properties that must be measured or found using tests include density, mass, volume, solubility, magnetism, and conductivity.

Temperature

Temperature is a property that tells how hot or cold a thing is. **Temperature** also demonstrates how much **thermal energy** is in a thing. When an object is cold, it has very little thermal energy. For many substances, being hot makes the substance expand, while being cold makes it shrink. Temperature also tends to transfer from one object to another. For instance, when a cup is filled with ice and water, the ice and water exchange energy until they are the same temperature. The ice and water reach the same temperature eventually, usually resulting in the ice melting.

Mass and Weight

Mass is a measure of how much **matter** is in an object. **Mass** is usually measured by placing an object on a scale. The terms mass and weight are often used interchangeably, but they actually have different definitions. Mass is always the same for a specific object, but **weight** depends on other factors. For instance, 1,000 lb. car always has the same mass, but it would weigh different amounts depending on if the car were on Earth or on Mars, which has much lower gravity.

Volume and Density

Volume is a measure of the **size** of an object or how much space an object takes up. Volume affects several other factors like density. Density is the amount of **mass** (amount of matter) in a certain **volume**. The more matter there is, the more mass an object has. **Density** takes into account both the mass and volume of an object. For instance, an inflated balloon has very little mass in it, but it is fairly large. A watermelon is about the same size, but has much more mass in it, so the watermelon is denser than the balloon. Density is the reason things float or sink. One example is oil and water. Oil is usually thicker than water, but it is actually less dense. If you put oil and water in a cup, you can see that the oil always **floats** to the top. Another way of thinking about it is that the water is actually **sinking** in the oil.

Density of Water

Density is the **mass** (amount of matter) in a certain **volume**. The more **matter** there is, the more the object weighs. Most solids have more matter than the same volume of their liquids. This means that they are denser and sink in their own liquid. However, water is different. The molecules in ice are farther apart than they are in liquid water. That means that ice has less matter in it than the same volume of liquid water. Therefore, ice is less dense and floats in water.

Materials Denser than Water

Ships and other floating objects made of materials that are denser than water float because of the empty space they contain inside their hulls. A ship weighing 5,000 tons overall will displace 5,000 tons of water, but this weight of water will occupy a smaller volume than the ship itself. Once this amount of water has been displaced the ship will not sink any deeper into the water and will float. Archimedes' principle states that the buoyant force is equal to the weight of the water (or any other fluid displaced). The reason a solid piece of iron or a rock sinks is that it weighs more than the volume of water it displaces. For the same reason, because a helium-filled balloon is lighter than air it will rise until the air's density is reduced such that the volume of air displaced is the same as the volume of the balloon.

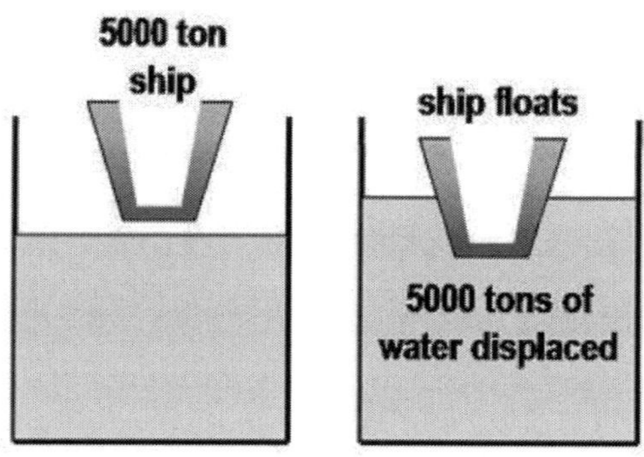

Density of Water and Ice

Most solids have more matter than the same volume of their liquids. This means that they are denser and sink in their own liquid. However, water is different. The molecules in ice are farther apart than they are in liquid water. That means that ice has less matter in it than the same volume of liquid water. Therefore, ice is less dense and floats in water.

Magnetism

Magnetism is a property that some rocks or metals can possess. **Magnetism** is a force that can push or pull on other magnetic materials. Magnets always have two poles, which attract the opposite pole and repel the same pole. Usually, the poles on a magnet are identified as being North or South, because the Earth's North and South Poles are actually magnetic as well. This is the reason that compasses work. The small needle in a compass is attracted to the Earth's poles and points in that direction. Many types of technology use magnetism, including electronics, motors, credit cards, and others.

Magnets

A **magnet** is any object or material, such as iron, steel, or magnetite (lodestone), that can affect another substance within its **field of force** that has like characteristics. A magnetic field is mapped by invisible curved lines of force that attract magnets or certain metals like iron or nickel. A simple bar magnet has a south pole (S) at one end and a north pole (N) at the other. Each pole will attract the opposite pole of another magnet and repel the same pole. The north pole of a compass needle will point to the south pole of a magnet, while the south pole of the needle will be attracted to the north pole of the magnet.

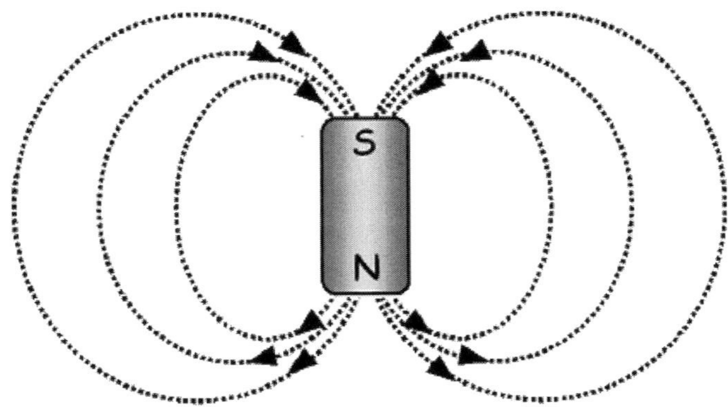

Opposite Poles of Two Magnets Attract Each Other

When two bar magnets are lined end to end with the north and south poles near each other, the lines of force run from the north pole of one magnet to the south pole of the other magnet indicating attraction.

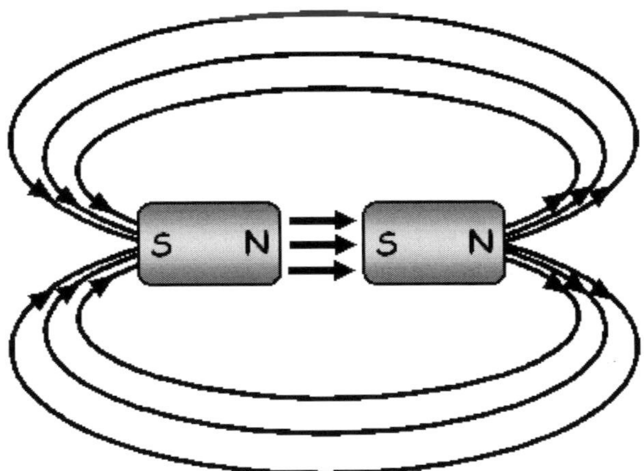

Cutting a Bar Magnet in Two

If a bar magnet is cut in two, two complete magnets will form, each with a north and south pole. If a bar magnet is cut it into three parts, three magnets will form.

Poles of Two Magnets Repel Each Other

When the like poles of two magnets are brought close to each other the lines of force run in opposite directions. This causes the two poles to push each other away.

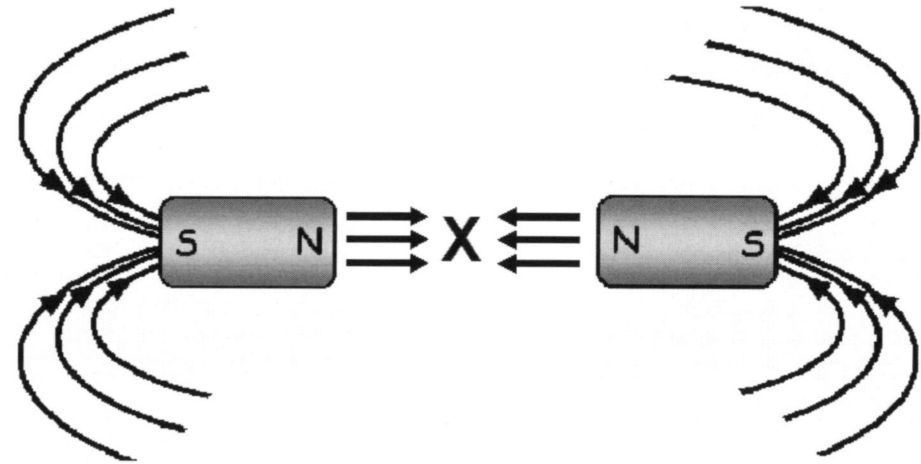

Needle of a Magnetic Compass

Planet Earth has a magnetic field just like a bar magnet. The north pole of a compass needle points to Earth's north pole because the magnetic pole near the North Pole is actually the south pole of Earth's magnetic field. Likewise, the south pole of the compass needle is attracted to the north pole of Earth's magnetic field near the south geographic pole. Just remember that each magnetic pole is attracted to its opposite pole on another magnet or magnetic object.

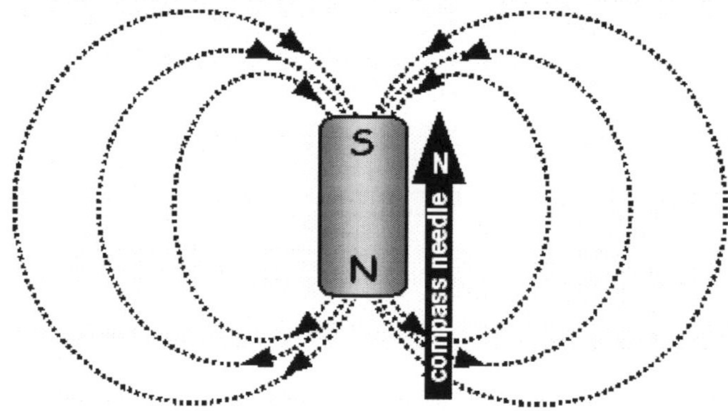

Conductivity

Conductivity is a property that describes how easily a material **transfers energy** to and from other materials. **Conductivity** usually refers to either heat energy or electrical energy. For instance, metals are usually good at conducting both heat and electricity, whereas plastic usually is not good at conducting these types of energy. Materials that are good at transferring energy are known as **conductors**, whereas materials that are not good at transferring energy are known as **resistors**.

Physical and Chemical Changes

Physical Changes

Physical changes are those that do not affect the chemical properties of a substance. Changes in state are **physical changes**. For example, a liquid can freeze into a solid or boil into a gas without changing the chemical nature of the substance. It is all still the same substance. Ice, steam, and liquid water are all still water, H_2O. Physical properties include such features as shape, texture, size, volume, mass, and density. Cutting, melting, dissolving, mixing, breaking, and crushing are all types of physical changes.

Chemical Changes

Chemical changes occur when chemical bonds are broken and new ones are formed. The original substances are **transformed** into different substances. If vinegar and baking soda are mixed together, a lot of bubbles (carbon dioxide) and water will form. Burning wood in a fireplace is another type of chemical change. The carbon in the wood reacts with oxygen in the air to make ash, carbon dioxide, smoke and energy that we feel as heat and see as light. When iron rusts, iron oxide is formed, indicating a chemical change. Other examples of chemical changes include baking a cake, digesting food, and mixing an acid and a base.

Examples of chemical changes include the following:

- (a) The temperature of a system changes without any heating or cooling.
- (b) The formation of a gas (bubbles).
- (c) The formation of a precipitate (solid) when two liquids are mixed.
- (d) A liquid changes color.

A **chemical change** occurs when two or more substances come together and interact in such a way that they become completely new substances. For example, two hydrogen atoms and one oxygen atom combine to make a new compound—a water molecule, H_2O. Likewise, two oxygen atoms and one carbon atom combine to make one molecule of carbon dioxide—CO_2. The two substances that combine are called **reactants,** and the new compound that emerges is the **product**. Chemical reactions (changes) can be much more complicated than this.

States of Matter

The three states of matter are solid, liquid, and gas. A **solid** has an exact shape and an exact volume. In a **solid**, the molecules are close together and locked into place. A **liquid** has an exact volume but does not have an exact shape. Because the molecules in a liquid move freely, liquids take the shape of their containers. Molecules in liquid have more space between them than molecules in solids do, but they do not move farther away from each other. A **gas** has no exact shape or volume. Gas particles are also free to move, and they move far away from each other so they can fill their containers. Gas particles usually have large spaces between them.

Solid	Liquid	Gas
Have a definite shape and size. Usually denser than liquids and gases of the same material.	Have a definite size, but do not have a definite shape.	Does not have a definite size or shape, but matches its container.
• Rocks • Ice Cream • Pencils • Apples	• Milk • Water • Juice • Rain	• Steam • Fire • Helium • Fog

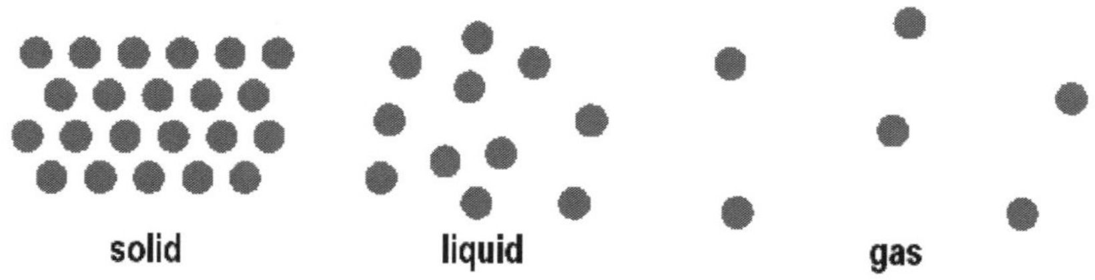

Review Video: States of Matter
Visit mometrix.com/academy and enter code: 742449

The following table shows similarities and differences between solids, liquids, and gases:

	Solid	Liquid	Gas
Shape	Fixed shape	No fixed shape (assumes shape of container)	No fixed shape (assumes shape of container)
Volume	Fixed	Fixed	Changes to assume shape of container
Fluidity	Does not flow easily	Flows easily	Flows easily
Compressibility	Hard to compress	Hard to compress	Compresses

PHASE STATES OF WATER

Water has three states of matter: ice, liquid water, and water vapor. Water freezes at 32 degrees Fahrenheit, where ice crystals form and the substance becomes a solid.

- **Ice** - Water crystalizes when it freezes, which means that it actually expands when it freezes, making it less dense than liquid water. This is uncommon because solids are usually the most dense form of a substance because the atoms are more tightly compressed. That is why ice actually floats in liquid water, rather than sinks.
- **Water Vapor** – Water exists in gas form as it evaporates or boils. Water vapor exists in the air and is often referred to as humidity. There is always some moisture in the air, though as the temperatures drop or pressure changes, it will condense and become liquid water again. Just like all other gas forms, water vapor spreads out in its container and flows much like a liquid.
- **Liquid Water** – Liquid water is the most common form on Earth. Water is needed for life and makes up most of the matter in a human body. Liquid water follows all of the typical rules for liquids, including taking the shape of its container, but has a constant mass and volume.

SIX DIFFERENT TYPES OF PHASE CHANGE

A substance that is undergoing a change from a solid to a liquid is said to be melting. If this change occurs in the opposite direction, from liquid to solid, this change is called freezing. A liquid which is being converted to a gas is undergoing vaporization. The reverse of this process is known as condensation. Direct transitions from gas to solid and solid to gas are much less common in everyday life, but they can occur given the proper conditions. Solid to gas conversion is known as sublimation, while the reverse is called deposition.

Review Video: Chemical and Physical Properties of Matter
Visit mometrix.com/academy and enter code: 717349

Review Video: States of Matter [Advanced]
Visit mometrix.com/academy and enter code: 298130

Mixture, Solution, and Colloid

A **mixture** is made of two or more substances that are combined in various proportions. The exact proportion of the constituents is the defining characteristic of any mixture. There are two types of mixtures: homogeneous and heterogeneous. **Homogeneous** means that the mixture's composition and properties are uniform throughout. Conversely, **heterogeneous** means that the mixture's composition and properties are not uniform throughout.

Solutions and Solubility

A **solution** is a homogeneous mixture of substances that cannot be separated by filtration or centrifugation. Solutions are made by dissolving one or more solutes into a solvent. For example, in a solution of sugar and water, sugar is the solute and water is the solvent. If there is more than one liquid present in the solution, then the most prevalent liquid is considered the solvent. The exact mechanism of dissolving varies depending on the mixture, but the result is always individual solute ions or molecules surrounded by solvent molecules. The proportion of solute to solvent for a particular solution is its **concentration**. Not all materials are able to be dissolved. Sugar is considered **soluble** in water, but sand does not dissolve in water, so it is considered **insoluble** in water.

A **colloid** is a heterogeneous mixture in which small particles (<1 micrometer) are suspended, but not dissolved, in a liquid. As such, they can be separated by centrifugation. A commonplace example of a colloid is milk.

Physical Properties of Mixtures and Solutions

When making a mixture or solution of ingredients, a person is not making a chemical change to the ingredients. Since the original ingredients are still present, their **physical properties** are usually still observable in the final mixture. Take, for instance, a solution of salt and water. The salt dissolves completely in the water, but since the salt is still present, the solution then tastes salty. Other properties, such as magnetism, do not transfer to the whole mixture. If a person were to mix sand and iron filings, then wave a magnet over the mixture, the iron filings would separate out, leaving only sand behind.

Motion and Stability – Forces and Interactions

Motion and Force

Sir Isaac Newton observed three major laws that explain motion. The term **motion** refers to the movement of an object. The term **force** refers to physical energy that is applied to an object. Newton referred to objects that are not moving as being in a state of **rest**.

- **Newton's First Law of Motion** - a body will remain at **rest** or in **motion** until a **force** is applied to it.
  - A bowling ball continues to roll in the same direction it was thrown until friction eventually slows it down.
  - A ball sitting on the ground will not move unless a force is applied to it.
  - A wagon will remain still until it is pulled by a person or an animal.
- **Newton's Second Law of Motion** - the amount of **acceleration** is determined by the amount of **force** and the **mass** of the object being moved.
  - A soccer ball will accelerate more if it is kicked harder.

  - A shopping cart is much easier to push than a car because it has much less mass than a car does.

- **Newton's Third Law of Motion** – For every **action**, there is an equal and opposite **reaction**.
    - The floor applies force upward to hold up the weight of a person standing on the floor.
    - A dog pulls against a leash that its owner is holding.

Directions of Motion

Motion can be linear, rotational, or oscillating.

- **Linear motion** – motion in a single direction, such as a bowling ball rolling down the lane or a train moving in one direction down its tracks
- **Rotational motion** – rotating or spinning in a circular motion, such as a top spinning, a merry-go-round, or the Earth rotating around the Sun
- **Oscillating motion** – bouncing up and down repeatedly, such as a yo-yo on a string, the motion of a spring, or the rising and falling of waves

Mass and Strength of Force

An object with a large mass can be moved by strong forces, but may not be moved by a weak force. However, a weak force may move an object with little mass very easily. In general, a strong force will have a greater effect on an object than a weak force will.

Gravity

Gravity is a force that exists between all objects with matter. **Gravity** is a **pulling** force between objects. This means that the forces on the objects point toward and pull toward the opposite object. Gravity is the force that the Earth applies to objects to pull them toward the center of the Earth.

Technically, all matter pulls other matter. The more mass an object has, the more it pulls. The Earth is seen as our center of gravity because it is the most massive object near humans. Gravity is also the reason that the Earth and other planets revolve around the Sun. The Sun is so massive that the Earth and all of the other bodies within the solar system are drawn to it and revolve around it.

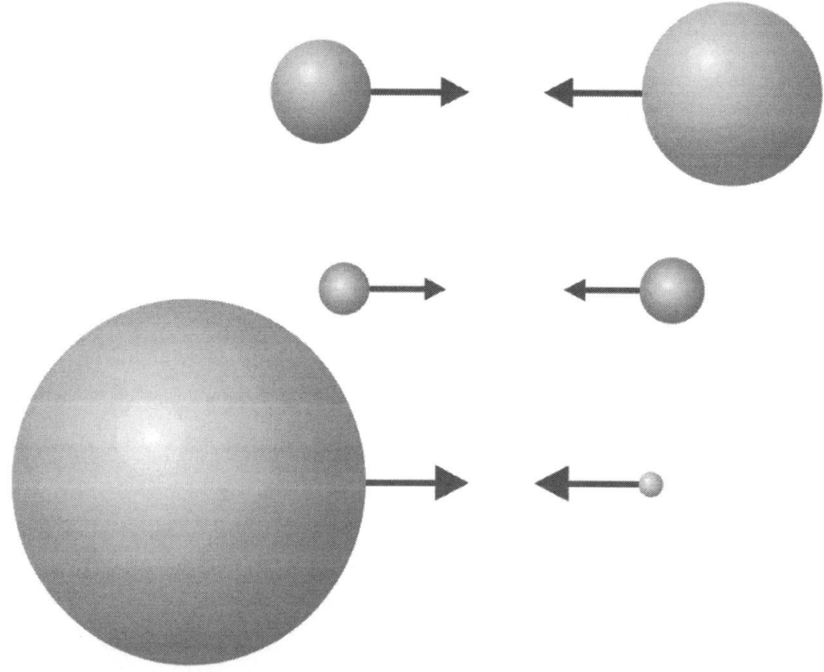

Forces Working Against Gravity

The direction of a force being applied to an object can impact the effect of the force. When force is applied to an object, it may be working against gravity. This means that the force must be **stronger** than gravity in order to move the object. If an object is on a flat surface, the pulling force used to lift it must be stronger than gravity, or the object will not be lifted. However, if an object is hanging from something, little force will be needed to pull it down because gravity is also working to pull it down. If an object is resting on an **incline**, gravity will be working to pull the object down the inclined surface. A pull from the higher side of the surface will not move the object unless it is stronger than gravity. Likewise, a push from the lower side of the surface will not move the object unless it is stronger than gravity. Objects on steeper inclines require more force to be moved.

Friction

Friction is **resistance** to motion between surfaces that are touching. In general, objects covered by or sitting on **rough** surfaces experience increased friction when moved. Objects covered by or sitting on **smooth** surfaces experience little friction when moved. To understand the concept of friction and force, imagine a book resting on a table. As it sits, the force of its weight is equal to and opposite of the normal force, which is the force pushing up against the book from the table. If a force was exerted on the book, such as in an attempt to push it to one side, friction force would oppose the motion. The friction force would be equal to and opposite the force of the push. This kind of friction force is called **static friction force**.

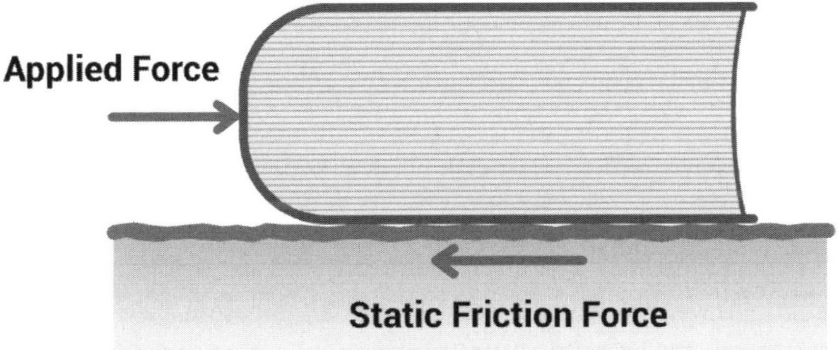

As the force on the book increases and overcomes the static friction force, the book will eventually accelerate in the direction of the pushing force. At this point, the friction force opposing the push becomes **kinetic friction force** because it is opposing kinetic energy. Often, the strength of the kinetic friction force is less than the strength of the static friction force. Because of this, the amount of force needed to keep moving the book will usually be less than the force needed to start moving the book.

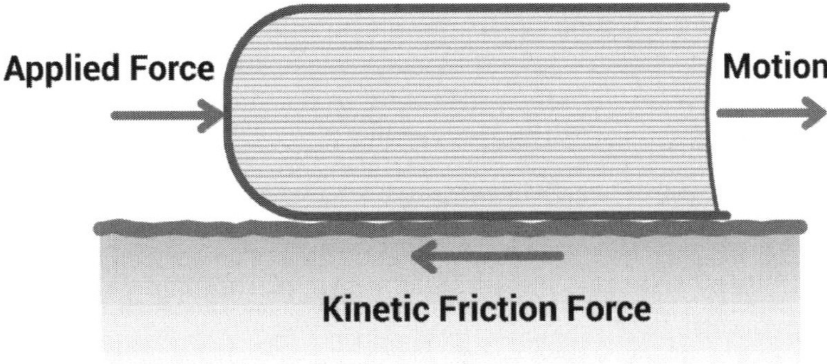

INERTIA, FRICTION, AND GRAVITY

When objects move, they keep moving until another force stops or changes its motion. This is called **inertia** or momentum. The heavier an object, the more inertia that object has. If there were no gravity or friction, an object in motion would go on moving in the same direction forever. In rotational motion, the mass of the object spinning has what is called rotational motion. Therefore, an object that is spinning, such as a spinning top, also carries momentum and would continue to spin forever if no other force were present. When a ball is rolled on the ground, the gravity of the Earth pulls the ball to the ground, which causes the ball to rub against the earth and cause friction. Instead of rolling forever, the friction slows the ball to a stop.

SPEED

Speed measures the distance an object moves in a certain amount of time. For instance, if a car is moving at a speed of 65 miles per hour, then that car will travel 65 miles in one hour. To calculate average speed, you can divide the total distance traveled over the time that has passed: **speed = distance / time**. For example, consider the speed of a runner who runs an 800-meter race in 2 minutes. To calculate the runner's average speed, use the following formula:

speed = distance / time

800 meters / 2 minutes

400 m/min

When dividing two different units, such as meters and minutes, the units of the answer calculated will reflect the original units of the numerator and denominator. Example units for speed include miles per hour (mi/hr or mph), kilometers per hour (km/hr or km/h), or meters per second (m/s).

BALANCED FORCES

An object is in equilibrium when the sum of all forces acting on the object is zero. When the forces on an object sum to zero, the object does not accelerate. Equilibrium can be obtained when forces in the y-direction sum to zero, forces in the x-direction sum to zero, or forces in both directions sum to zero.

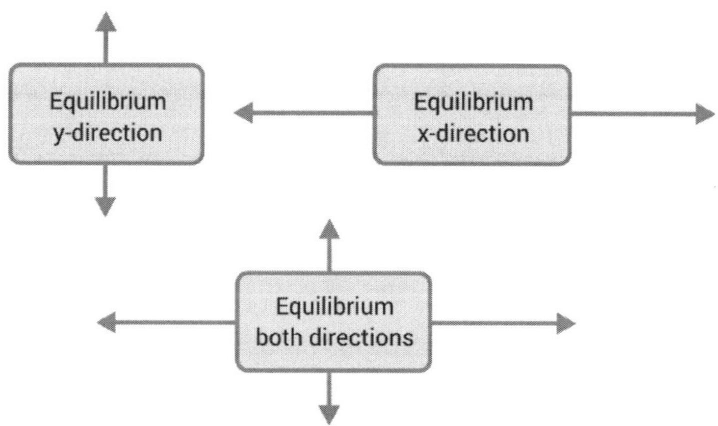

In most cases, a problem will provide one or more forces acting on an object and ask for a force to balance the system. The force will be the opposite of the current force or sum of current forces.

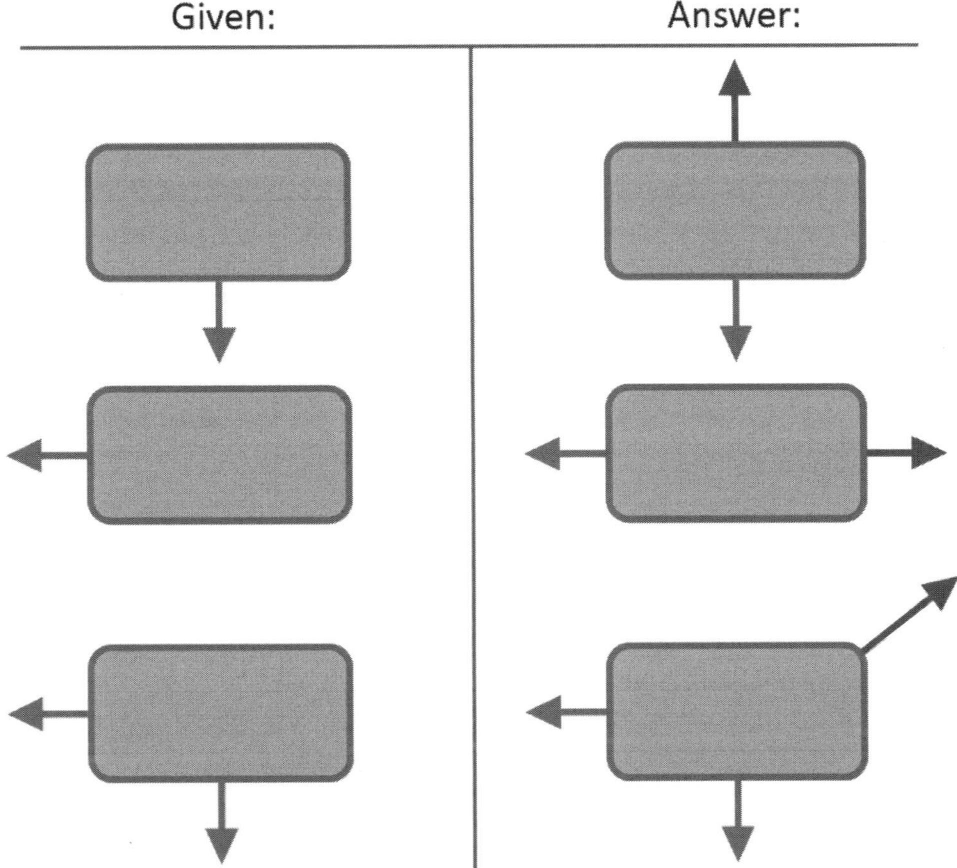

Life Science

From Molecules to Organisms – Structures and Processes

Organizational Hierarchy within Multicellular Organisms

Cell theory states that all organisms are made of cells, that cells are the basic unit of biological life, and that all cells arise from other cells. In **multicellular** organisms, cells combine to create different physiological structures with specific functions. There are four levels of organization in the human body: cells, tissues, organs, and organ systems. Different types of **cells** make up **tissues**. For example, muscle cells make up muscular tissue. Tissues make up **organs** with specific functions, such as the brain, heart, or liver. Organs work together as **organ systems**, such as the digestive system or the cardiovascular system. Organ systems are complex networks that achieve processes necessary to sustain life, such as breathing, moving, or eating.

Cells

Cells are the basic structural units of all living things. Cells are composed of various molecules including proteins, carbohydrates, lipids, and nucleic acids. All animal cells are eukaryotic and have a nucleus, cytoplasm, and a cell membrane. Organelles include mitochondria, ribosomes, endoplasmic reticulum, Golgi apparatuses, and vacuoles. Specialized cells are numerous, including but not limited to, various muscle cells, nerve cells, epithelial cells, bone cells, blood cells, and cartilage cells. Cells are grouped to together in tissues to perform specific functions.

Membrane-Bound Organelles

Prokaryotic cells are much simpler than eukaryotic cells. Prokaryote cells do not have a nucleus due to their small size and their DNA is located in the center of the cell in a region referred to as a **nucleoid**. Eukaryote cells have a **nucleus** bound by a double membrane. Eukaryotic cells typically have hundreds or thousands of additional **membrane-bound organelles** that are independent of the cell membrane. Prokaryotic cells do not have any membrane-bound organelles that are independent of the cell membrane. Once again, this is probably due to the much larger size of the eukaryotic cells. The organelles of eukaryotes give them much higher levels of intracellular division than is possible in prokaryotic cells.

Review Video: Cell Structure
Visit mometrix.com/academy and enter code: 591293

Cell Walls

Not all cells have cell walls, but most prokaryotes have cell walls. The cell walls of organisms from the domain Bacteria differ from the cell walls of the organisms from the domain Archaea. Some eukaryotes, such as some fungi, some algae, and plants, have cell walls that differ from the cell walls of the Bacteria and Archaea domains. The main difference between the cell walls of different domains or kingdoms is the composition of the cell walls. For example, most bacteria have cell walls outside of the plasma membrane that contains the molecule peptidoglycan. **Peptidoglycan** is a large polymer of amino acids and sugars. The peptidoglycan helps maintain the strength of the cell wall. Some of the Archaea cells have cell walls containing the molecule pseudopeptidoglycan, which differs in chemical structure from the peptidoglycan but basically provides the same strength to the cell wall. Some fungi cell walls contain **chitin**. The cell walls of diatoms, a type of yellow algae, contain silica. Plant cell walls contain cellulose, and woody plants are further strengthened by lignin. Some algae also contain lignin. Animal cells do not have cell walls.

Chromosome Structure

Prokaryote cells have DNA arranged in a **circular structure** that should not be referred to as a chromosome. Due to the small size of a prokaryote cell, the DNA material is simply located near the center of the cell in a region called the nucleoid. A prokaryotic cell may also contain tiny rings of DNA called plasmids. Prokaryote cells lack histone proteins, and therefore the DNA is not actually packaged into chromosomes. Prokaryotes reproduce by binary fission, while eukaryotes reproduce by mitosis with the help of **linear chromosomes** and histone proteins. During mitosis, the chromatin is tightly wound on the histone proteins and packaged as a chromosome. The DNA in a eukaryotic cell is located in the membrane-bound nucleus.

Cells and Organelles of Plant Cells and Animal Cells

Plant cells and animal cells both have a nucleus, cytoplasm, cell membrane, ribosomes, mitochondria, endoplasmic reticulum, Golgi apparatus, and vacuoles. Plant cells have only one or two extremely large vacuoles. Animal cells typically have several small vacuoles. Plant cells have chloroplasts for photosynthesis and use this process to produce their own food, distinguishing plants as **autotrophs**. Animal cells do not have chloroplasts and therefore cannot use photosynthesis to produce their own food. Instead animal cells rely on other sources for food, which classifies them as **heterotrophs**. Animal cells have centrioles, which are used to help organize microtubules and in in cell division, but only some plant cells have centrioles. Additionally, plant cells have a rectangular and more rigid shape due to the cell wall, while animal cells have more of a circular shape because they lack a cell wall.

Review Video: Difference Between Plant and Animal Cells
Visit mometrix.com/academy and enter code: 115568

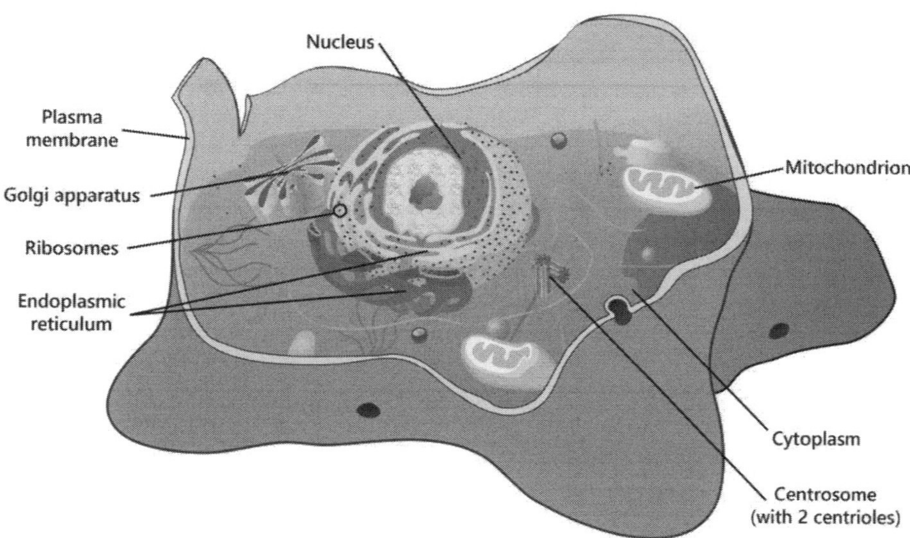

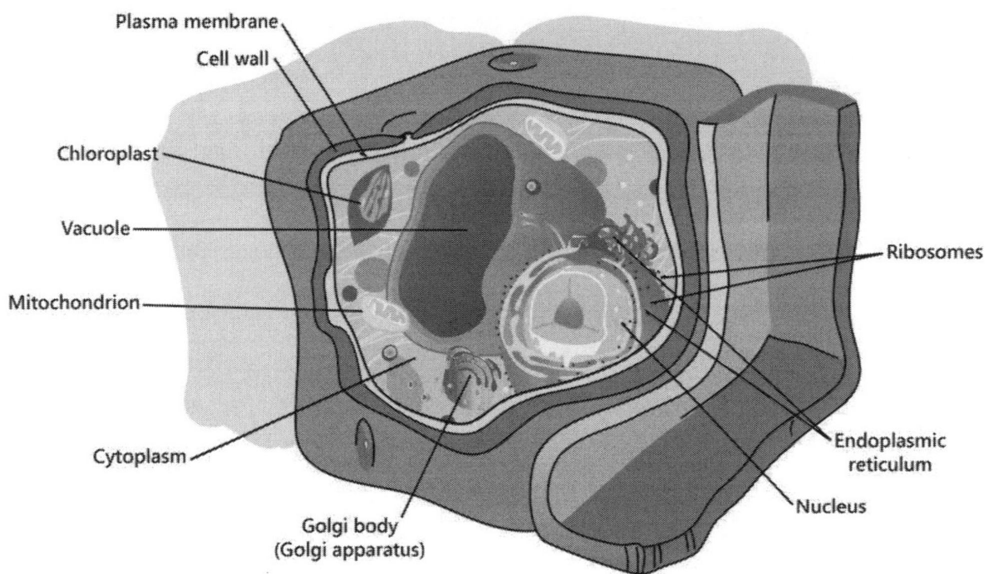

Cell Membranes

The **cell membrane**, also referred to as the plasma membrane, is a thin semipermeable membrane of lipids and proteins. The cell membrane isolates the cell from its external environment while still enabling the cell to communicate with that outside environment. It consists of a phospholipid bilayer, or double layer, with the hydrophilic ("water-loving") ends of the outer layer facing the external environment, the inner layer facing the inside of the cell, and the hydrophobic ("water-fearing") ends facing each other. Cholesterol in the cell membrane adds stiffness and flexibility. Glycolipids help the cell to recognize other cells of the organisms. The proteins in the cell membrane help give the cells shape. Special proteins help the cell communicate with its external environment, while other proteins transport molecules across the cell membrane.

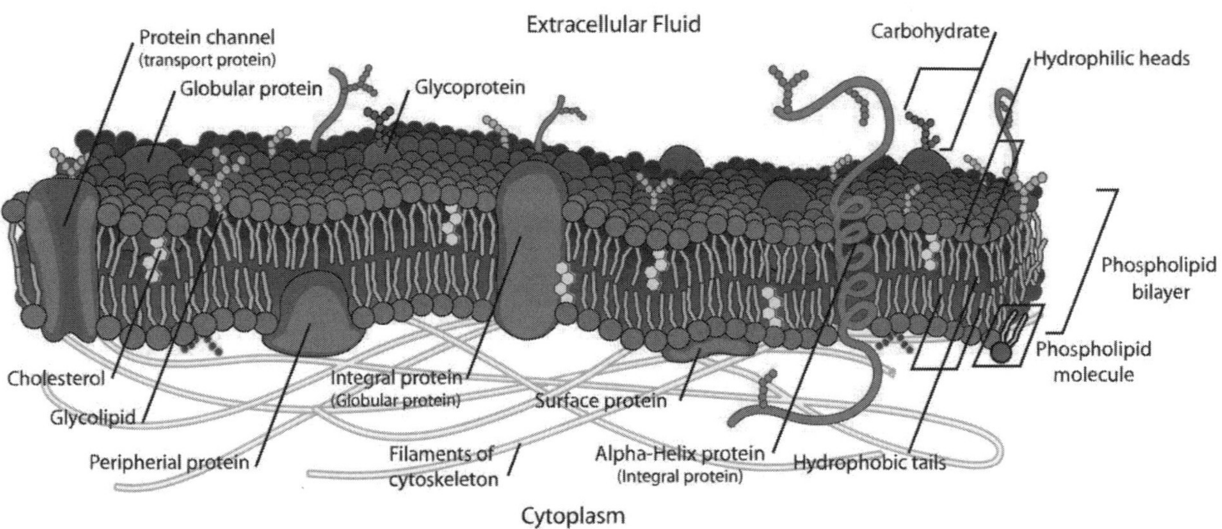

Review Video: Function of the Plasma Membrane
Visit mometrix.com/academy and enter code: 943095

Nucleus

Typically, a eukaryote has only one nucleus that takes up approximately 10% of the volume of the cell. Components of the nucleus include the nuclear envelope, nucleoplasm, chromatin, and nucleolus. The **nuclear envelope** is a double-layered membrane with the outer layer connected to the endoplasmic reticulum. The nucleus can communicate with the rest of the cell through several nuclear pores. The chromatin consists of deoxyribonucleic acid (DNA) and histones that are packaged into chromosomes during mitosis. The **nucleolus**, which is the dense central portion of the nucleus, produced and assembles ribosomes with the help of ribosomal RNA and proteins. Functions of the nucleus include the storage of genetic material, production of ribosomes, and transcription of ribonucleic acid (RNA).

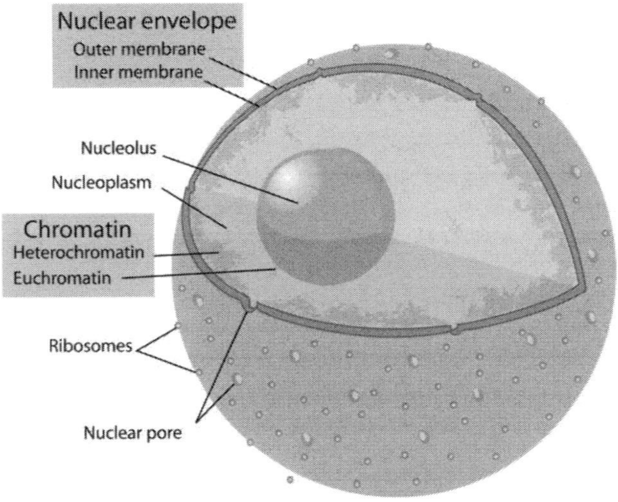

Chloroplasts

Chloroplasts are large organelles that are enclosed in a double membrane. Just as cells contain a fluid called cytoplasm, chloroplasts contain a fluid called the **stroma**. Within the stroma, there are discs called **thylakoids**, which are arranged in stacks called grana (singular: granum). The thylakoids have chlorophyll molecules on their surfaces. **Stromal lamellae** separate the thylakoid stacks. Chloroplasts perform photosynthesis and make food (in the form of sugars) for the plant. The light reaction stage of photosynthesis occurs in the grana, and the dark reaction stage of photosynthesis occurs in the stroma. Sugars are formed in the stroma. Chloroplasts have their own DNA and can reproduce by fission independently.

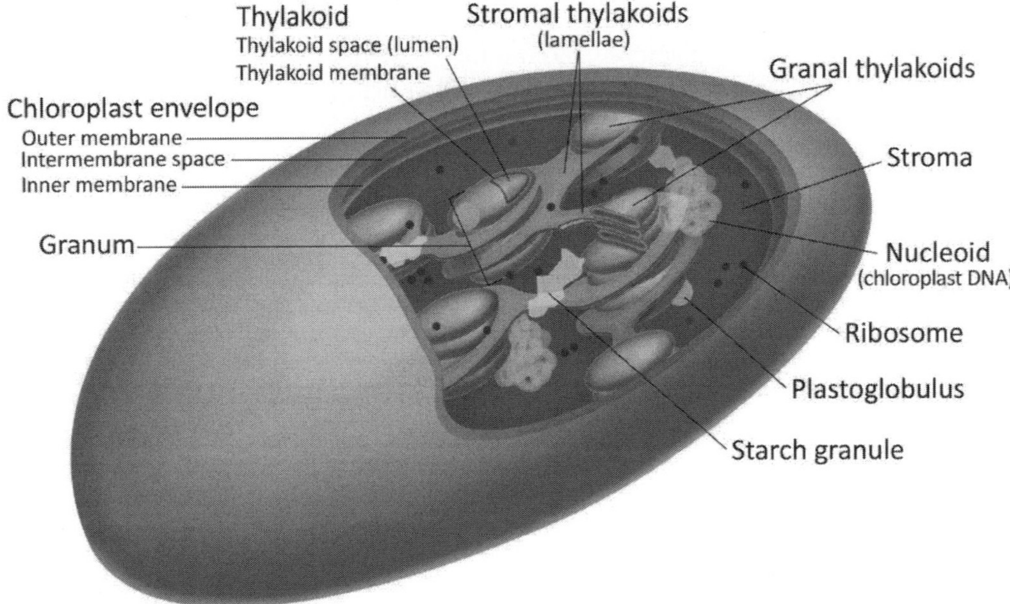

MITOCHONDRIA

Mitochondria break down sugar molecules and produce energy in the form of molecules of adenosine triphosphate (ATP). Both plant and animal cells contain mitochondria. Mitochondria are enclosed in a bilayer semi-membrane of phospholipids and proteins. The intermembrane space is the space between the two layers. The **outer membrane** has proteins called porins, which allow small molecules through. The **inner membrane** contains proteins that aid in the synthesis of ATP. The matrix consists of enzymes that help synthesize ATP. Mitochondria have their own DNA and can reproduce by fission independently. Mitochondria also help to maintain calcium concentrations, form blood components and hormones, and are involved in activating cell death pathways.

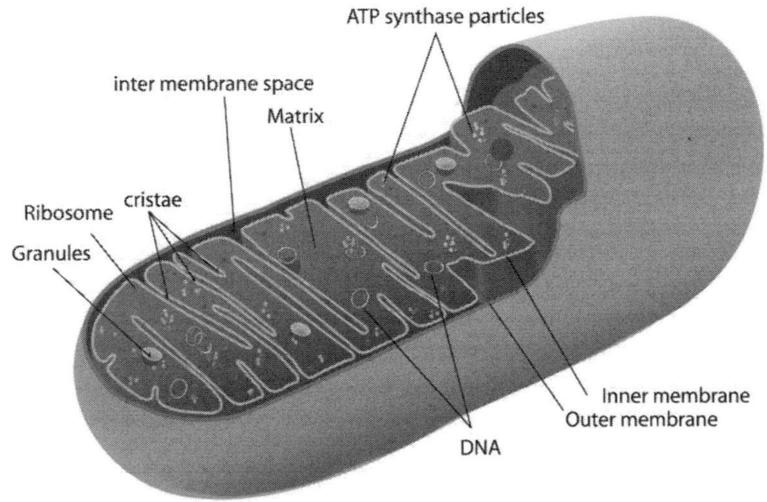

Review Video: Mitochondria
Visit mometrix.com/academy and enter code: 444287

RIBOSOMES

A **ribosome** consists of RNA and proteins. The RNA component of the ribosome is known as ribosomal RNA (rRNA). Ribosomes consist of two subunits, a large subunit and a small subunit. Few ribosomes are free in the cell. Most of the ribosomes in the cell are embedded in the rough endoplasmic reticulum located near the nucleus. Ribosomes are protein factories and translate the code of DNA into proteins by assembling long chains of amino acids. **Messenger RNA** (mRNA) is used by the ribosome to generate a specific protein sequence, while **transfer RNA** (tRNA) collects the needed amino acids and delivers them to the ribosome.

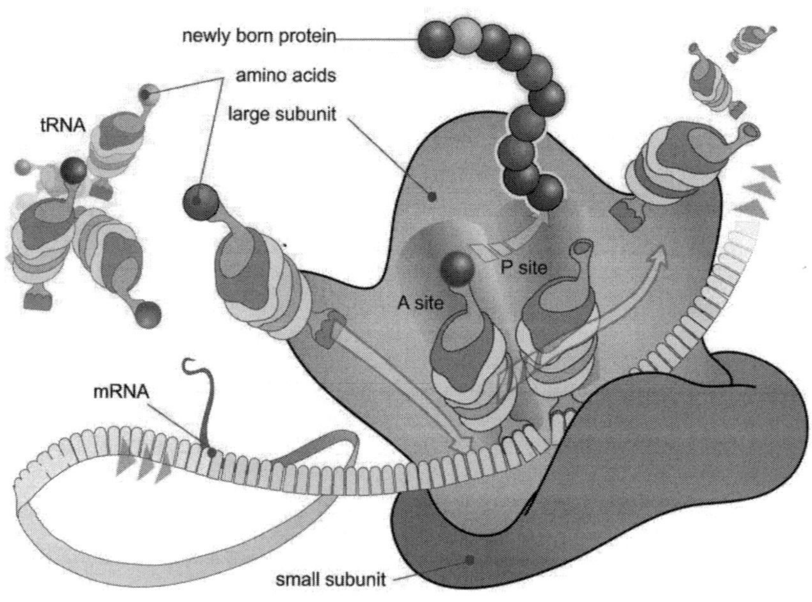

Golgi Apparatus

The **Golgi apparatus**, also called the Golgi body or Golgi complex, is a stack of flattened membranes called **cisternae** that package, ship, and distribute macromolecules such as carbohydrates, proteins, and lipids in shipping containers called **vesicles**. It also helps modify proteins and lipids before they are shipped. Most Golgi apparatuses have six to eight cisternae. Each Golgi apparatus has four regions: the cis region, the endo region, the medial region, and the trans region. Transfer vesicles from the rough endoplasmic reticulum (ER) enter at the cis region, and secretory vesicles leave the Golgi apparatus from the trans region.

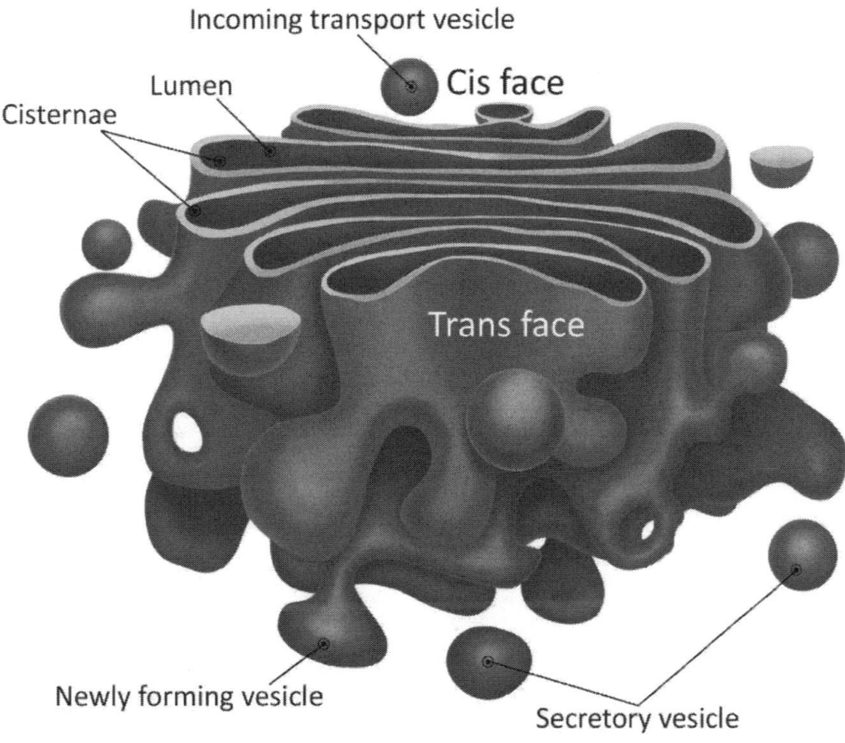

CYTOSKELETON

The **cytoskeleton** is a scaffolding system located in the cytoplasm. The cytoskeleton consists of elongated organelles made of proteins called microtubules, microfilaments, and intermediate filaments. These organelles provide shape, support, and the ability to move. These structures also assist in moving the chromosomes during mitosis. Microtubules and microfilaments help transport materials throughout the cell and are the major components in cilia and flagella.

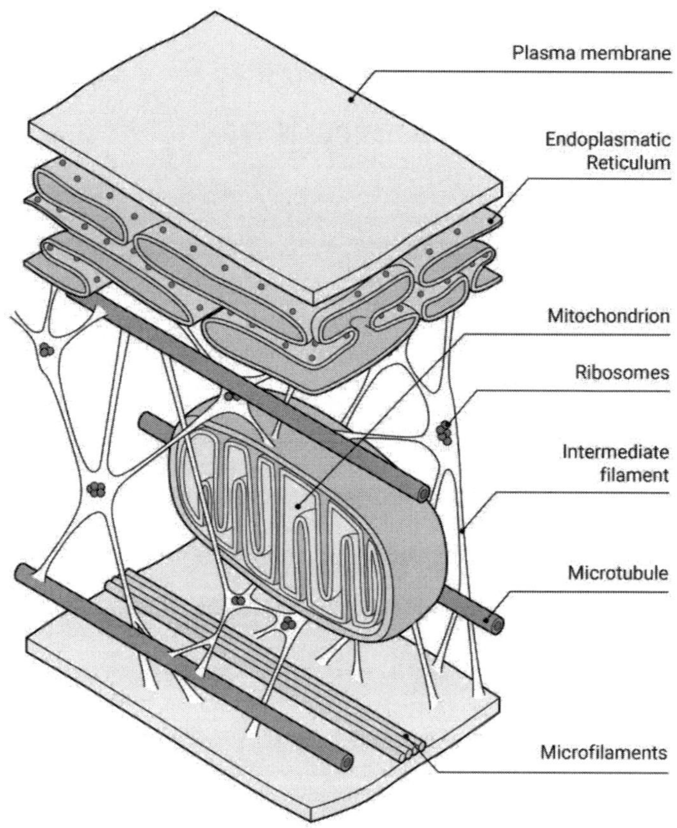

TISSUES

Tissues are groups of cells that work together to perform a specific function. Tissues can be grouped into four broad categories: muscle tissue, connective tissue, nerve tissue, and epithelial tissue. Muscle tissue is involved in body movement. **Muscle tissues** can be composed of skeletal muscle cells, cardiac muscle cells, or smooth muscle cells. Skeletal muscles include the muscles commonly called biceps, triceps, hamstrings, and quadriceps. Cardiac muscle tissue is found only in the heart. Smooth muscle tissue provides tension in the blood vessels, controls pupil dilation, and aids in peristalsis. **Connective tissues** include bone tissue, cartilage, tendons, ligaments, fat, blood, and lymph. **Nerve tissue** is located in the brain, spinal cord, and nerves. **Epithelial tissue** makes up the layers of the skin and various membranes. Tissues are grouped together as organs to perform specific functions.

Organs and Organ Systems

Organs are groups of tissues that work together to perform specific functions. **Organ systems** are groups of organs that work together to perform specific functions. Complex animals have several organs that are grouped together in multiple systems. In mammals, there are 11 major organ systems: integumentary system, respiratory system, circulatory system, endocrine system, nervous system, digestive system, excretory system, muscular system, skeletal system, reproductive system, and immune system.

1. **Integumentary system:** the protective barrier of the body, including skin, hair, and nails.
2. **Respiratory system:** responsible for allowing air to enter and exit the lungs to obtain oxygen and release carbon dioxide. The respiratory system consists of the nasal passages, pharynx, larynx, trachea, bronchial tubes, lungs, and diaphragm.
3. **Circulatory system:** includes the heart, blood, and blood vessels that carry blood through the body, delivering oxygen to tissues.
4. **Endocrine system:** manages and releases hormones responsible for bodily functions and behavior, including hunger, stress, sleep, and many others. The endocrine system consists of several ductless glands, which secrete hormones directly into the bloodstream.
5. **Nervous system:** includes your brain, spinal cord, sense organs, and nerves. The nervous system allows you to sense, process, and respond to external stimuli. It also helps regulate physiological and behavioral processes.
6. **Digestive system:** processes and extracts nutrients from food. The excretory system is responsible for removing waste following digestion. The digestive system includes the stomach, intestines, liver, gallbladder, pancreas, and anus.
7. **Excretory system:** metabolizes food, filters blood, and excretes waste. It includes the kidneys and bladder.
8. **Muscular system:** includes muscles that allow the body to move. The muscles work in combination with the skeletal system.
9. **Skeletal system:** includes the bones, joints, and cartilage that make up your skeleton.
10. **Reproductive system:** enables humans to produce offspring. It includes the external and internal reproductive organs.
11. **Immune System:** keeps a record of microbes to recognize and destroy the microbes that enter your body and make you feel sick. It includes white blood cells, antibodies, complement system, lymphatic system, spleen, bone marrow, and thymus.

Ecosystems – Interactions, Energy, and Dynamics

Abiotic Factors and Biotic Factors

Abiotic factors are the nonliving physical and chemical factors in the environment. Even though they are not living, the growth and survival of living organisms depend on abiotic factors. These factors can determine the types of plants and animals that will establish themselves and thrive in a particular area. Some abiotic factors, such as oxygen, sunlight, and water, are taken in by organisms. Other abiotic factors are not taken in by organisms, but organisms still need them for shelter and protection from harm. Abiotic factors include:

- Light intensity available for photosynthesis
- Temperature range
- Available moisture
- Types of rocks
- Types of minerals

- Types of atmospheric gases
- Relative acidity (pH) of the system

Biotic factors are the living components of an environment. Biotic factors affect the relationships between organisms and the available resources in an area, which can limit the type and number of resident species. Predator/prey, producer/consumer, and parasite/host relationships can define a community. Biotic factors include:

- Population levels of each species
- Food requirements of each species
- Interactions between species
- Wastes produced

EXAMPLE

Which of these situations describes an interaction between living and nonliving parts of an ecosystem?

a. A coyote preys upon rabbits
b. A deer eats leaves and berries
c. A mountain lion drinks water from a stream
d. An animal avoids eating a cactus because of its spikes

Choice A is an example of a predator eating its prey. Because the question is asking for an example of an interaction between living and nonliving parts of an ecosystem, one of the factors here needs to be a nonliving part of the animal's physical environment. Coyotes and rabbits are both living things, so this answer can be eliminated.

Choice B is an example of an herbivore eating plants. Plants are living things, so this does not describe a relationship between living and nonliving factors. Choice B is incorrect.

Choice C describes an animal, the mountain lion, drinking water from a stream. Water is a nonliving thing that animals need to survive, so this answer could be correct.

Choice D is an example of a plant protecting itself from an herbivore, in this case with spikes. Both animals and cacti are alive, so this choice can be eliminated.

Choice C describes an example of an animal relying on an aspect of its physical environment, making this an example of an interaction between living and nonliving parts of an ecosystem. Choice C is the correct answer.

PRODUCERS, CONSUMERS, AND DECOMPOSERS

Producers are organisms that can make their own food. Most producers are plants. Plants use sunlight, carbon dioxide from the air, and water to make sugars that provide **energy** through a process called **photosythesis**. Plants only need sunlight, water, and certain minerals and other nutrients to live, grow, and reproduce. **Consumers** are organisms that eat other organisms. **Decomposers** are organisms that feed on decaying plant and animal matter. Since decomposers cannot make their own food, they are classified as consumers. Fungi, such as mushrooms, are decomposers. They break down the tissues and wood of living or dead plants or the bodies of dead animals.

Energy Pyramid

Energy flows through an ecosystem as producers and consumers are consumed by other organisms. The flow of energy can be tracked through an energy pyramid. An **energy pyramid** shows how energy is transferred from one trophic level to another. **Trophic levels** describe whether an organism is a producer or a consumer and how much energy is typically passed to them when they eat. Producers always form the **base** of an energy pyramid, and the energy they pass along comes from the **Sun**. Consumers form successive levels above the producers. Producers only store about 1% of the solar energy they receive. Then, each successive level only uses about 10% of the energy of the previous level. Therefore, **primary consumers** use about 10% of the energy used by primary producers, such as grasses and trees. Next, **secondary consumers** use 10% of the energy used by primary consumers, or 1% overall. This continues up for as many trophic levels as exist in a particular ecosystem.

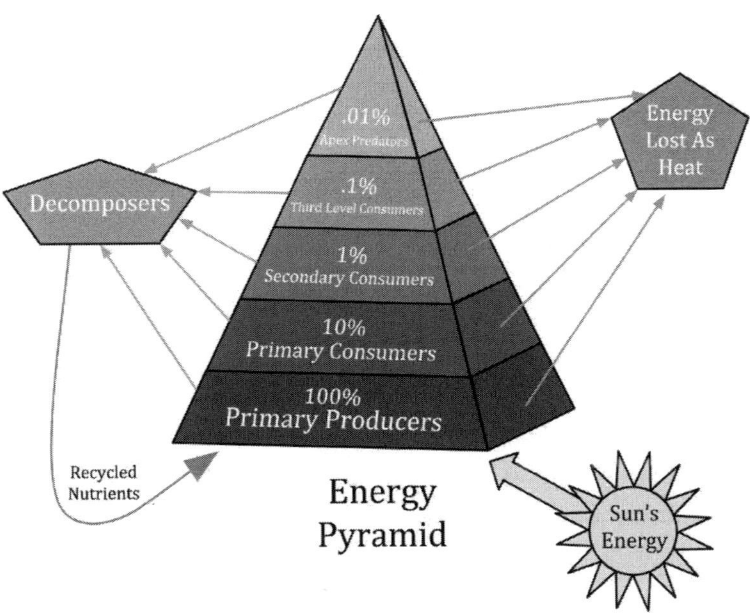

FOOD WEB

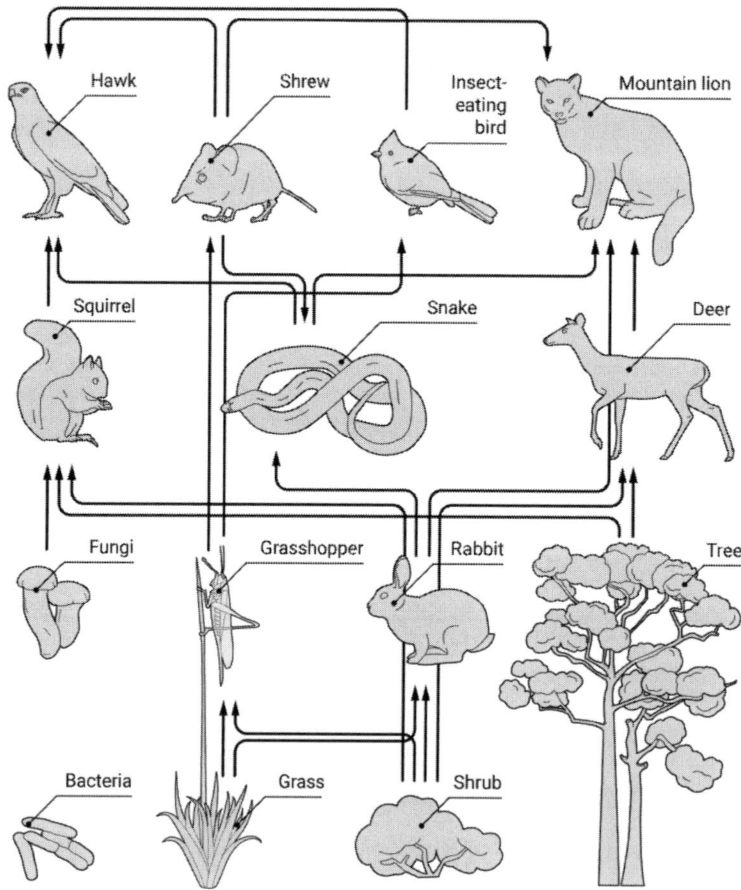

Energy flow through an ecosystem can also be illustrated by a **food web**. Energy moves through the food web in the direction of the arrows. In the food web above, **producers** such as grass, trees, and shrubs use energy from the Sun to produce food through photosynthesis. **Herbivores** or **primary consumers** such as squirrels, grasshoppers, and rabbits obtain energy by eating producers. **Secondary consumers**, which are carnivores such as snakes and shrews, obtain energy by eating the primary consumers. **Tertiary consumers**, which are carnivores such as hawks and mountain lions, obtain energy by eating the secondary consumers.

Review Video: Food Webs
Visit mometrix.com/academy and enter code: 853254

INTERDEPENDENCE OF THE FOOD WEB

Because each level of consumer is dependent on the previous level for food, the population of each level affects the other animal groups. For instance, if an ecosystem is made up of only grass, deer, and wolves, grass is the producer, the deer eat the grass, and the wolves eat the deer. If deer are overhunted one year, the grass is given more room to grow because less of it is consumed. However, the wolves will not have enough food, so the wolf population will reduce in size. Eventually, because of the abundance of grass and a reduced population of wolves, the deer may then have a surge in population the next year. This example is not a realistic example, as there are usually many more producers, consumers, and predators within an ecosystem.

Example

Which of the following accurately depicts the first three steps in the movement of energy through an ecosystem?

a. Sun → producers → consumers
b. Producers → Sun → consumers
c. Consumers → producers → decomposers
d. Decomposers → consumers → producers

Choice A depicts the movement of energy from the Sun to producers and then to consumers. Producers get energy from the Sun through photosynthesis, while consumers get energy by eating plants or other animals. The path depicted in Choice A matches this pattern, so Choice A could be the correct answer.

Choice B depicts energy moving from producers to the Sun and then to consumers. Producers such as plants gain energy from the Sun, so the Sun should come first in this pathway. Choice B is incorrect.

Choice C describes the movement of energy from consumers to producers and then to decomposers. Producers get energy from the Sun while consumers eat other living organisms, so producers should always come before consumers in an energy pathway. Choice C is not the answer.

Choice D depicts the movement of energy from decomposers to consumers and then to producers. Decomposers get energy by breaking down the remains of plants and animals that have died, recycling nutrients into the ecosystem. Decomposers cannot be the first step in energy transfer, so Choice D is incorrect.

Choice A is the correct answer because it accurately shows the movement of energy from the Sun to producers through photosynthesis, followed by consumers that eat other living organisms.

Food Web in a Pond

Sunlight allows green algae to photosynthesize and grow. The algae are fed upon by small animals like water fleas and copepods. In turn, these are eaten by small worms, mosquito larvae and other larval insects. These are then eaten by mosquito fish, which in turn are eaten by larger fishes like bluegills. The bluegills are preyed upon by even larger fishes like bass and by herons, egrets and raccoons (which also eat the bass). Then the animal waste and everything that dies and settles to the bottom is decomposed by bacteria and fungi.

Food Web in a Meadow

Sunlight allows grass and other plants to grow. These plants are eaten by a variety of *herbivores* like insects, rodents, and rabbits. Their seeds are consumed by various birds such as sparrows and quail. The insects are eaten by *carnivores*, including other kinds of birds, shrews, and bats. The rodents, rabbits, and some of the birds are then eaten by larger carnivores like weasels and foxes. Also, the quail, mice, rabbits and shrews are eaten by owls at night and by hawks during the day.

Competition Between Different Organisms

Animals and plants have to compete with other species for food or nutrients, water, places to live, nesting or breeding sites, sunlight in the case of plants, and other factors in the environment that may be scarce or limited. In addition, animals and plants of the same species have to compete with each other for these resources and for the opportunity to breed and reproduce. Competition may seem harmful to some plants and animals, but it actually helps some species. Competition helps control population sizes and prevents **overpopulation**. Overpopulation of a species can be dangerous since there may not be enough resources to support all of the animals of that species or animals of other species.

CHANGES TO ECOSYSTEMS

Most ecosystems rely on **consistent patterns** and a **balance** between organisms and resources. When something changes this balance, the ecosystem may suffer. For example, consider a grassland ecosystem. Deer are grazers, animals that eat grass, and they have natural predators, such as wolves. If something happens and the predators of the deer disappear, the ecosystem may suffer. The deer would likely become overpopulated because fewer deer would be hunted by the predators. This would become a problem because as the population grows, there may not be enough grass in the area to feed all of the deer and all of the other animals that eat grass. As a result, grass may become scarce and other animals, such as insects, would lose their habitats since there would be little grass. This situation shows that even one change can hurt many members of an ecosystem.

Humans can also harm ecosystems. For example, when a new road or building is created, it takes up land that had grass, trees, bushes, or other plants growing on it. These plants provide shelter, food, and fresh oxygen for many animals. When these resources are removed, the animals must find them elsewhere. This not only harms the original ecosystem, but it can also harm the ecosystems the animals move to. The animals can cause too much competition in the new ecosystems if there are not enough resources to provide for the new animals and the animals that were already there. If this occurs, organisms from both the old and new populations could suffer.

TRAITS AND ENVIRONMENTS

Each organism has **traits** that affect that organism's ability to **survive**. Some of these traits are common among different species that live in similar environments. For example, many desert animals have traits that help them either survive on a small amount of water or extract water from their surroundings. A trait may also help an organism obtain food or shelter in its environment. For example, flamingos have beaks that are shaped in a way that allows flamingos to find food underwater. Furthermore, flamingos have webbed feet so they can easily live in shallow water. Woodpeckers have beaks that are shaped in a way that allows them to find food under tree bark. In addition, they have talons so they can hold onto tree limbs and build nests. These traits help both species of bird survive in their environments.

TRAITS FOR WARDING OFF PREDATORS

Many organisms have traits that protect them from predators. For example, an animal's hair color or skin color may help it blend in with its surroundings and hide. Some animals have skin that can hurt or taste bad to predators, which can lead predators to avoid trying to eat that animal. Many of these traits are the result of **adaptations**, or traits that species developed over time to help them live in their environment.

EXAMPLE

Which traits would make a species more successful in an aquatic environment?

a. A beak
b. Webbed feet
c. A tail
d. Opposable thumbs

Choice A suggests a beak, which could be useful in obtaining certain types of food. A trait that would make a species more successful in an aquatic environment should be specifically related to living in water. A beak would probably be more useful on land, so Choice A is incorrect.

Choice B suggests webbed feet. Webbed feet could be useful in an aquatic environment because the extra skin between the animal's toes could be helpful for swimming. Additionally, webbed feet are unlikely to be helpful in non-aquatic environments. Choice B could be the correct answer.

Choice C suggests a tail, which is common in animals that live in many habitats, not just in the water. Choice C is not the correct answer.

Choice D suggests opposable thumbs such as those found in humans and other primates. Opposable thumbs allow animals to use tools and do things with their hands, which would be more helpful on land than in the water. Choice D is incorrect.

Choice B, webbed feet, is the only trait that is specifically related to an animal's success in an aquatic environment, making it the correct answer.

Biome

A **biome** is a region that includes the plants and animals best suited to the soil type and climate in an area. This concept is related to the relationships between organisms and their environment. Since plants are more abundant than animals, biomes are often described based on the type of vegetation that exists in the older ecosystems within the biome. Though the word *biome* only refers to the living things in an area, each type of biome is associated with a certain climate. When looking at where the different types of biomes are located around the world, a pattern can be observed. A biome type may appear on different continents, but across those continents, the areas where that biome appears will be located at similar **latitudes**. This is because each type of biome is closely related to certain climate and soil types, and similar climates and soil types tend to appear at similar latitudes.

Savanna Biome

The **savanna biome** is often found near the edge of an **equatorial rainforest**, which is a type of rainforest that exists near the equator. The savanna biome is commonly found in regions that experience a wet-dry tropical climate. During the dry season, the lack of moisture in the soil causes trees in the savanna biome to grow with much space between them. This allows a dense lower layer of grasses and other plants to grow. Though fire is fairly common in savannas during the dry season, the vegetation in these regions tends to be quite fire resistant. In fact, many geographers believe that such fires prevent rainforest vegetation from overrunning the savanna biome.

Grassland Biome

The **grassland biome** is commonly subdivided into two types: tall-grass prairie and steppe. The **tall-grass prairie** type of grassland does not have trees and has much tall grass and broad-leaved herbs called forbs. This kind of biome usually forms in regions with distinct summer and winter seasons, in subtropical or midlatitude climates. The **steppe, or short-grass prairie,** type of grassland is known for having scattered clumps of short grasses and the occasional shrub or small tree. Many grass species and forbs populate this kind of region. Steppes are usually found in midlatitude areas with dry continental climates. In steppes, vegetation grows in wet spring months and becomes dormant during dry summer months.

DESERT BIOME

The **desert biome** may be subdivided into two types: semidesert and dry desert. The **semidesert** type of desert is found at a wide range of latitudes. It is characterized by thinly-spaced shrubs that have adapted to survive in arid climates. **Steppe regions** may be converted to semidesert through events such as a high number of cattle moving through the area, which tread upon and consume regional vegetation. The thorn-tree semidesert is found in the tropical zone, and has a long, dry hot season and a short, severe rainy season. Thorny vegetation (such as cacti), called thorn-bush or thorn-woods, populate the thorn-tree semidesert.

The **dry desert subdivision** is even barer than the semidesert. Only tough plants that have adapted to live in the climate, such as cacti and hard grasses, can survive under desert conditions. Many dry desert areas display no plant life at all. This is due to the sand that covers the ground, which does not allow for conditions that help plants grow.

TUNDRA BIOME

The **tundra biome** may be subdivided into two types: arctic or alpine. The **arctic tundra** exists at very high latitudes near the poles. During the brief summer season in these areas, low vegetation such as herbs, mosses, and grasses are able to grow because above-freezing air temperatures allow the surface layer to melt. The type and number of plant species depends on the moisture levels in the (usually frozen) ground during the warm season. In the cold season, frost action snaps roots in the ground. Freezing wind and snow kill plants above the ground. **Alpine tundra** is located at high elevations, above the tree line and below bare mountain tops. Physically, the alpine tundra is quite similar to the arctic tundra.

FOREST BIOMES

The **forest biome** has an abundance of soil and moisture and has warm temperatures for a portion of the year. Trees are the dominant vegetation type in this biome. There are many different types of forest biomes:

- **Low-latitude rainforests** exist in equatorial and tropical climate zones. They contain many different species of tall, densely-spaced trees, normally with broad leaves. The canopy created by this vegetation casts shade on the ground below, which limits the growth of plants on the bottom layer.
- **Monsoon forests** may also be found in tropical latitude zones. However, this type of forest exists in regions that experience a wet season and a dry season. During these seasons, many tree species lose their leaves. This allows the vegetation on the lower layer of the forest to grow.
- **Subtropical evergreen forests** have fewer, shorter tree species than low-latitude rainforests. They also include a lush lower layer of vegetation.
- **Midlatitude deciduous forests** are common in regions of the northern hemisphere that have distinct seasons. During the warm summer season, the tall trees in this type of forest form a nearly closed canopy. In the winter season, these trees lose their leaves. The lower level vegetation also varies with the season, as they grow in the spring and die out when the dense upper canopy forms in the summertime.
- **Needleleaf forests** are made up largely of conifers. Many trees in this type of forest are evergreen, meaning that they shed their leaves once every several years. The spacing of the trees in this forest class may be dense, preventing the growth of vegetation on the ground.

LANDFORMS

DELTAS, CANYONS, AND DUNES

A **delta** is landform that is created where a river flows into a larger body of water. The river carries sediment. When it reaches the larger body of water, the water from the river spreads out and the sediment is deposited. Sediment is **deposited** by a river when the movement of the river causes it to move to a different area and it is able to fall through the water and settle. An example is the Mississippi Delta, where the Mississippi River meets the Gulf of Mexico. A **canyon** is a deep ravine between two cliffs. Canyons are usually formed by erosion caused by flowing water over extended periods of time. An example of this is the Grand Canyon in Arizona. A **sand dune** is a mound of sand built by a natural force, such as wind, over time. Forces like wind can create sand dunes by moving grains of sand until they form a mound. Great Sand Dunes National Park, located in Colorado, is home to the tallest sand dunes in the United States.

EXAMPLE

The Grand Canyon, located in Northern Arizona, is the largest canyon in the United States. It reaches a maximum of 6,000 feet deep. Which of the following factors is most likely to be responsible for the formation of the Grand Canyon?

a. Erosion by water and wind
b. Cracking of the soil resulting from hot and dry weather
c. Accumulation of sediment on the sides of the river
d. Tectonic plate movement

Choice A proposes that the Grand Canyon was formed through erosion and weathering. Over very long periods of time, water and wind can have drastic effects on a landscape and even wear away at rock. Choice A could be correct.

Choice B proposes that the Grand Canyon was formed from soil cracking due to hot weather. While this does happen in certain types of soil, it would not be forceful enough to create such a large canyon. Choice B is not the answer.

Choice C proposes that the sediment carried by the river accumulated on both sides, creating the high walls of the canyon. While this is true for the creation of most riverbanks, this process would not be able to create the enormous heights of the Grand Canyon's walls. Choice C can be eliminated.

Choice D proposes that the Grand Canyon is the result of tectonic plate movement. While tectonic plate movement is likely responsible for the formation of the high ground or plateau that the canyon cuts through, it would not have created the canyon itself. This choice is incorrect.

Choice A proposes the best explanation for the formation of the Grand Canyon, which was formed through the effects of moving water over the course of a very long period of time.

GLACIERS

Glaciers start high in the mountains, where snow and ice accumulate inside a cirque (a small semicircular depression). The snow becomes firmly packed into masses of coarse-grained ice that are slowly pulled down a slope by gravity. Glaciers grow with large amounts of snowfall and retreat (diminish) if warm weather melts more ice than can be replaced. Glaciers once covered large areas of both the northern and southern hemispheres with mile-thick ice that carved out valleys, fjords, and other land formations. They also moved plants, animals, and rocks from one area to another. There were two types of glaciers: **valley**, which produced U-shaped erosion and sharp-peaked mountains; and **continental**, which moved over and rounded mountain tops and ridges. These glaciers existed during the ice ages, the last of which occurred from 2.5 million years ago to 12,000 years ago.

Mountains

A **mountain** is a portion of the Earth that has been raised above its surroundings by volcanic action or tectonic plate movement. Mountains can be made of any type of rock and most lie along active plate boundaries. There are two major mountain systems. The **Circum-Pacific** encircles the entire Pacific Ocean, from New Guinea up across Japan and the Aleutians and down to southern South America. The **Alpine-Himalaya** stretches from northern Africa across the Alps and to the Himalayas and Indonesia. **Orogeny** is the term for the process of natural mountain formation. Therefore, physical mountains are orogens. **Folded mountains** are created through the folding of rock layers when two crustal plates come together. The Alps and Himalayas are folded mountains. The latter was formed by the collision of India with Asia. **Fault-block mountains** are created from the tension forces of plate movements. These produce faults that vertically displace one section to form a mountain. **Dome mountains** are created from magma pushing up through the Earth's crust.

Oceans, Seas, Lakes, Rivers, and Canals

- **Oceans** are the largest bodies of water on earth and cover nearly 71% of the earth's surface. There are five major oceans: Atlantic, Pacific (largest and deepest), Indian, Arctic, and Southern (surrounds Antarctica).
- **Seas** are smaller than oceans and are somewhat surrounded by land like a lake, but lakes are fresh water and seas are salt water. Seas include the Mediterranean, Baltic, Caspian, Caribbean, and Coral.
- **Lakes** are bodies of water in a depression on the earth's surface. Examples of lakes are the Great Lakes and Lake Victoria.
- **Rivers** are a channeled flow of water that start out as a spring or stream formed by runoff from rain or snow. Rivers flow from higher to lower ground, and usually empty into a sea or ocean. Great rivers of the world include the Amazon, Nile, Rhine, Mississippi, Ganges, Mekong, and Yangtze.
- **Canals** are artificial waterways constructed by humans to connect two larger water bodies. Examples of canals are the Panama and the Suez.

Heredity – Inheritance and Variation of Traits

Inherited Traits and Learned Behaviors

Plant and animal characteristics and behaviors can be inherited or learned. An **inherited trait** is **genetic**, or passed to the organism by its parents, and is present at birth. For an animal, this could be eye color, fur type, skin color, or hair color. For a plant, this could be the color, pattern, or shape of a leaf or flower. Inherited traits in plants could also be the size and shape of seeds or features such as thorns or spines. A **learned behavior** is something that an organism learns to do in order to survive. These behaviors are learned by observing other animals and through repeated outcomes. When organisms learn to care for the young and protect each other, they have gained a learned behavior. A bird learning how to build a nest or an animal learning the best places to build a habitat are also examples of learned behaviors. Another example of a learned behavior is when an animal is trained to do something, such as a pet dog standing near the door when it wants to go outside.

Animal Migration

Many animals make a regular two-way, long-distance journey due to seasonal changes affecting the availability of food, weather or rainfall. Birds are especially noted for this, but other animals like bats, some butterflies, moths, and grasshoppers also migrate back and forth between northern winter and southern summer territories. Caribou and wildebeest also make spectacular migrations. The figure at right shows the 14,000-mile migration route of the Swainson's hawk, which spends its summers in western North America and winters in South America.

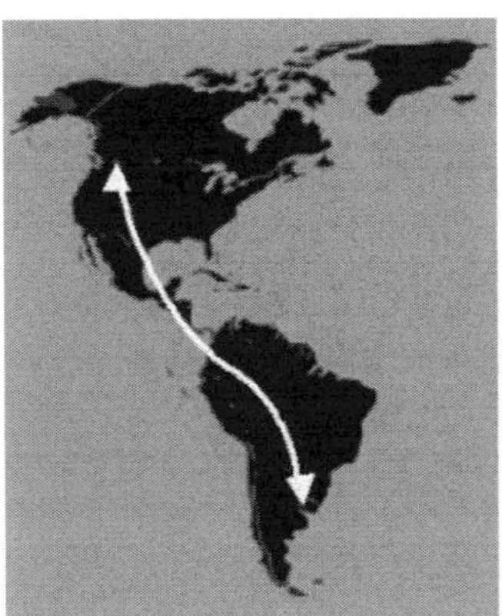

Learned Behaviors in Animals

Many behaviors in higher animals such as birds and mammals actually have to be learned. Bird songs are usually learned. Male cardinals sing slightly different songs in different areas of the country. They learn these dialects from the adult birds around them. Also, unlike the instinctive migration of spawning salmon, sandhill cranes must be taught the long migration routes they fly between their nesting and winter grounds. Likewise, most predatory mammals must learn how to hunt from their mothers.

Instinctive Behaviors

Instinctive behaviors are actions that are automatic in an animal and do not have to be taught or learned. Newly hatched sea turtles automatically crawl across the beach towards the ocean with no mother around to show them what to do. Tree squirrels automatically store acorns and nuts during the summer in order to have food in the coming winter. Also, salmon automatically return from the ocean to the freshwater river where they hatched in order to spawn.

Hibernation

Hibernation occurs when an animal enters a state of inactivity in which its body temperature drops, and its breathing and metabolism slow down, and it goes into a deep sleep for many days, weeks, or even months. This allows animals to survive long, cold winters when food is scarce. Bears, ground squirrels and other rodents, some bats like the one shown hibernating here, and certain kinds of snakes are known to hibernate. Some animals sleep through hot summer weather or droughts. This is called *aestivation*.

EXAMPLE

Which of these traits could be inherited from an animal's parents?

a. A dog learning to sit
b. A cat begging for food every morning
c. The shape of a bird's beak
d. A hamster that is overweight

Choice A describes a dog learning a trick, specifically to sit on command. Inherited traits show up naturally and do not need to be prompted or learned. If the dog had puppies, the puppies would not automatically know how to sit on command because this behavior is not passed down from parents to offspring. Choice A is incorrect because it is a learned behavior rather than an inherited trait.

Choice B describes a cat that begs for food every morning. While the cat was probably not taught to beg, this is a behavior that the cat learned by discovering that begging would lead to getting something they want. This is another example of a learned behavior that would not have been automatically passed down from the cat's parents. Choice B is not the answer.

Choice C has to do with a physical trait, specifically the shape of a bird's beak. Physical traits such as the shape of an animal's body parts are typically inherited directly from an animal's parents. Choice C could be the correct answer.

Choice D involves a physical trait of a hamster's weight. While some animals might be more prone to becoming overweight than others, inheritance is not the only factor affecting an animal's weight. The hamster's food consumption and activity level likely also played a role in its weight, eliminating Choice D as the correct answer.

Choice C, the shape of a bird's beak, is the only trait that can be fully inherited and is not affected by the animal's environment or developed as a learned behavior. Choice C is the correct answer.

Earth and Space Science

Earth's Systems

Weather and Climate

Weather describes conditions or changes in sunshine, temperature, cloud coverage, precipitation, warm and cold fronts, and more during a specific time in a specific area. These components can change throughout a day, week, or month. Meteorologists track and report what is happening in the atmosphere to help predict how the weather will change in the near future. Weather data is collected and studied over long periods of time, often multiple decades, to evaluate the climate of a particular area. **Climate** refers to patterns in weather conditions, such as temperature, precipitation, and any extremes related to them, in a specific area over a very long period of time. A large factor that influences climate is latitude, which is the distance of an area from the equator.

Clouds

Clouds form when water vapor in the atmosphere cools to the point where it **condenses** and becomes water droplets or small particles of frozen ice crystals. Clouds form when moisture is added to the air through evaporation until the air becomes **saturated** and cannot hold any more water. Then, the water vapor can condense into visible droplets.

Precipitation

Precipitation is water that falls back to the surface of the Earth from the atmosphere. This water may be in the form of **rain**, which is water in liquid form. Raindrops are formed in clouds due to **condensation**. When the drops become too large to remain in the clouds, gravity causes them to fall toward the surface of the Earth. Extremely small raindrops are called **drizzle**. If the temperature of a layer of air through which rain passes is below the freezing point of water, the rain may take the form of **sleet**, which is partially frozen water. Precipitation may also fall in the form of **snow**, which is made of ice crystals. When clumps of snowflakes melt and refreeze, **hail** is formed. Hail may also be formed when liquid water gathers on the surface of a snowflake and then freezes.

Temperature

Temperature describes the amount of **heat** in an area. The Earth's tilt and shape impact the average temperatures in each region. The Sun shines on the areas closest to the equator most directly, causing those areas to have warmer average temperatures. All other areas receive energy from the Sun at different angles, causing lower average temperatures. The farther North or South an area is from the equator, the less directly the Sun will shine on them. Since temperature is an important part of the water cycle, it also has an effect on the humidity, precipitation, and air pressure in an area. Since weather processes are like cycles, these factors can also impact the temperature in an area. Temperature can be predicted based on an area's location, the time of year, the moisture in an area, and the air pressure in an area.

Air Pressure

Pressure describes the amount of force applied to an object over a certain area. For example, a person standing on a bed sinks deeper into the bed than a person laying on it. This occurs because the same amount of force is applied to a smaller area, which means the pressure is higher. Pressure applies to all forces that are applied to other objects, including air. The pressure applied by air in a given place is called **air pressure**, or **barometric pressure**. Because air has mass, and gravity is pulling it toward the Earth, air applies force on everything beneath it. Air pressure changes with

altitude, which is the height of an object above sea level. The lower the altitude, the higher the air pressure. This is because the air at higher altitudes is weighing on the air underneath it. Similarly, air pressure is lower at higher altitudes.

Impact of Temperature and Humidity on Air Pressure

Humidity and temperature also affect air pressure. **Humidity** refers to how much moisture is in the air. Air that contains more water molecules contains more mass than drier air. Therefore, gravity pulls more on air that has higher humidity, which causes increased air pressure. Similarly, **temperature** can affect the density of air. Gases do not have a constant volume, but the space between the molecules in a gas grows and shrinks with changes in temperature, causing changes in air pressure.

Impact of Air Pressure on Climate and Weather

Weather systems are often described based on air pressure. A **high-pressure system** means that an area has higher air pressure, while a **low-pressure system** has a lower pressure. Pressure will move toward **equilibrium**, or a state of **balance**. Therefore, high- and low-pressure systems naturally interact with each other. Low pressure systems try to **pull air** toward them to reach equilibrium. This causes condensation to form and can eventually produce storms. High pressure systems **push air** away from them and are usually associated with sunny or clear weather.

Weather Fronts

An **air mass** is a region of air that has a consistent temperature and amount of moisture throughout. A **front** is the boundary that usually forms between an air mass and the air surrounding it. This boundary may be sloped or vertical. The shape of the boundary depends on the movement of the air masses that it runs between. There are four types of fronts:

- A **cold front** occurs when a cold air mass moves into an area of warmer air. In this situation, the colder, denser air mass remains near the ground, pushing the warmer mass upward. When the ascending air is unstable, this movement may create severe weather, such as thunderstorms.
- A **warm front** is formed when a warm air mass enters an area of colder air. The warmer air ascends, causing precipitation.
- An **occluded front** occurs when a cold air mass moves past a moving mass of warm air near the surface of the Earth. A cold air mass will usually move more quickly than a warm air mass because it has a higher density. The coldest air remains near the ground, forcing the warmer air to rise.
- A **stationary front** forms when warm and cold air meet and neither air mass can apply enough force to move the other. They remain stationary.

LIGHTNING

Lightning is a huge electric spark that can occur inside a cloud, go from one cloud to another, or go from a cloud to the ground. Turbulent rising air and rising and falling raindrops or ice crystals in a thunderstorm cause differences in electric charge in different parts of the cloud and between the bottom of the cloud and the ground. When the difference in charge is large enough, a lightning bolt will discharge, which neutralizes the difference.

THUNDER

As a lightning bolt travels through the air, it pushes the air aside faster than the speed of sound. This produces a shock wave of extremely hot air that creates a loud sonic boom, which we hear as **thunder**. If a person can hear thunder, he or she needs to get indoors quickly as possible, since he or she could be struck by lightning.

We hear thunder later than lightning strikes because sound travels much slower than light. Light travels so fast that it is almost instantaneous from one point to another anywhere on Earth. Sound travels much more slowly—about one mile every five seconds. Light travels one mile in about 5 millionths of a second. Therefore, the approximate distance a person is from a lightning flash can be determined if he or she counts the number of seconds between when the lightning flashed and the thunder it made was heard.

TORNADO

A **tornado** is a violent rotating column of air that is in contact with both the ground and a cloud. The column is visible because the extremely low pressure causes water vapor to condense and become visible water droplets. Tornados usually stirs up clouds of dirt and debris when they touch the ground. Tornadoes are the most violent storms on Earth, and the strongest spin at 300 miles per hour.

HURRICANE

A **hurricane** is a large tropical storm that forms over the open ocean and produces very strong winds and heavy rains. A **tropical storm** forms when warm water evaporates and the saturated air rises and forms a column of condensed water vapor. As the wind speed increases the pressure falls even more and a hurricane can form. Sinking air in the center of the storm produces an **eye** (see the arrow in the image below) where the weather is quite calm and free of clouds.

MEASURING WEATHER

Weather can be measured using a variety of methods. Rainfall, sunshine, pressure, humidity, temperature, and cloudiness can be measured using tools such as **thermometers**, **barometers**, and **rain gauges**. However, the use of **radar** and **satellite imagery** allows meteorologists to observe at weather across large areas, such as entire continents. This helps meteorologists understand and make predictions about current and developing weather systems. **Infrared** (heat-sensing) **imaging** allows meteorologists to measure the temperature of clouds above ground. Using weather reports gathered from different weather stations spread over an area, meteorologists create **synoptic charts**. The locations and weather reports of several stations are plotted on a chart. Analysis of pressures, rainfall, cloud cover, and other factors reported from each location can reveal basic weather patterns.

Rapid Changes to the Earth's Surface

Normally, the Earth's surface changes with processes such as erosion, weathering, and the warming and cooling of the planet over time. Occasionally, the Earth encounters rapid changes that can be devastating to ecosystems. Examples of natural events that rapidly change the landscape include volcanoes, earthquakes, landslides, hurricanes, tornados, and wildfires.

- **Volcanoes** are mountains or hills that have passages to magma deep beneath the earth. Convection within the Earth's core can cause lava, rock, or gas to travel through these passages to the surface. Volcanoes can be active or dormant.
- **Earthquakes** are strong vibrations in the ground caused by movements in the Earth's crust.
- **Landslides** are sudden shifts of large amounts of land down a hill or mountain as a result of erosion, rain, earthquakes, or volcanic movement.
- **Hurricanes** are large, violent storms with wind and rain arising from warm waters in the ocean.
- **Tornados** are sudden, violent windstorms that can tear apart buildings in a matter of minutes. They often form without warning and usually happen when cold, dry air meets hot, humid air, causing rapid convection.
- **Wildfires** are large destructive fires that spread through woods and brush, destroying habitats. These usually occur in dry environments.

Water Cycle

The **water cycle** refers to the circulation of water in the Earth's hydrosphere. The **hydrosphere** exists below the surface, on the surface, and above the surface of the Earth. The water cycle is a process that involves five physical actions.

- **Evaporation** refers to liquid water heating up and changing to into a gas known as water vapor.
- **Transpiration** occurs when water inside plants evaporates directly out of plant leaves.
- **Condensation** refers to the water vapor cooling down and beginning to turn back into a liquid form, which causes clouds to form.
- **Precipitation** refers to rain, snow, hail, or sleet that falls from clouds once water vapor has condensed enough.

- The **storage** stage of the water cycle refers to water being stored in the ground, trees, or bodies of water on the Earth. Water is trapped in vegetation, collected in bodies of water on the Earth's surface, or absorbed into the Earth's surface. **Runoff**, caused by gravity, physically moves water downward into oceans or other water bodies.

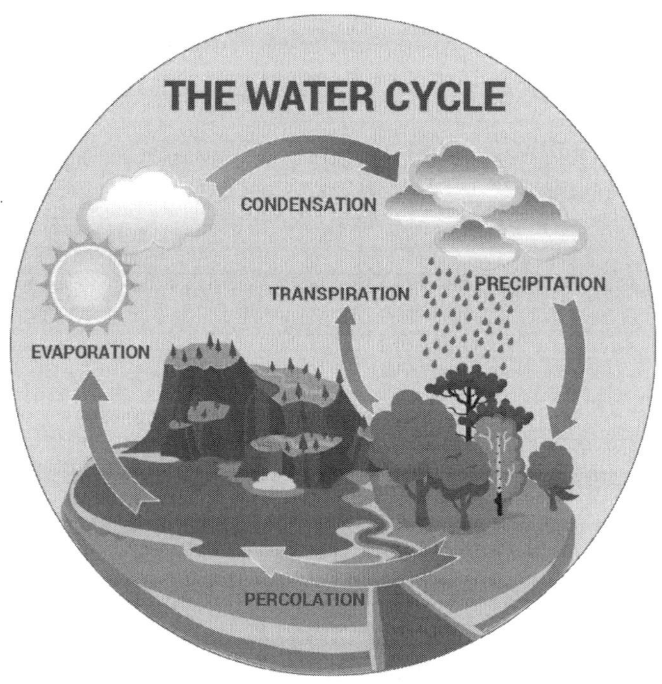

Review Video: Hydrologic Cycle
Visit mometrix.com/academy and enter code: 426578

Roles of the Sun and the Ocean in the Water Cycle

More than 96% of the Earth's water is in the oceans, and the oceans cover more than 70% of the Earth's surface. Ocean water plays a major role in the water cycle. The Sun is also extremely important to the water cycle because it heavily impacts the temperature of the water that sits on Earth's surface. As sunlight hits the surface of the ocean, water heats and begins to **evaporate**. It becomes **water vapor**, which is a gas. The water vapor rises into the atmosphere and **condenses** to form **clouds**. These clouds travel and move across the Earth due to air currents. As more water evaporates and condenses, the clouds become heavy and begin to **precipitate**. This results in **rain**, which collects on the Earth's surface and provides water for living things that need it to survive. These processes also help to regulate the Earth's temperature and prevent large changes in temperature.

Practice Test #1

1. Why are plants considered producers?

a. They make their own food
b. They soak up water from the ground
c. Their leaves can be large or small
d. They produce pollen, which is a food source for many insects and birds

2. Which statement accurately describes a state of matter?

a. Solids take the shape of their container
b. Gases maintain a fixed shape
c. Liquids will expand to fill the volume of a container
d. Gases expand to fill an entire space

3. A ball is resting on the front end of a boat. The boat is moving straight forwards toward a dock. When the front of the boat hits the dock, how will the ball's motion change?

a. The ball will remain at rest
b. The ball will move backwards
c. The ball will move forwards
d. The ball will move sideways

4. The Sahara desert receives about 3.6 inches of precipitation per year. Antarctica is also a desert receiving between 3 to 8 inches of precipitation per year. What makes an area a desert?

a. The temperature
b. The amount of animal life
c. The number of people living in the region
d. The yearly precipitation

5. In a food chain, where does energy go after the secondary consumer dies?

a. Back to the Sun
b. To the producers
c. Into air, becomes wind
d. To decomposers

6. How are organisms, such as snakes, cacti, and coyotes, able to survive in harsh desert conditions?

a. Over thousands of years these organisms have developed adaptations to survive in arid climates
b. These organisms migrate out of the desert during the summer months, only living in the desert for a portion of the year
c. Snakes, cacti, and coyotes work together to find sources of food and water
d. Snakes, cacti, and coyotes are all aquatic species that live in ponds and rivers during the hot day

7. How is force being applied to the box below?

BOX →

a. The box is being pulled forward
b. The box is being pushed forward
c. Gravity is forcing the box to move forward
d. Friction is forcing the box to stop

8. What is the benefit of a kangaroo's large ears?

a. They improve the kangaroo's vision
b. Large ears help kangaroos taste their food
c. Large ears allow kangaroos to outrun predators
d. Large ears help kangaroos hear predators coming

9. The teacher challenges a pair of students to decide the best way to separate an unidentified mixture with only the information given below.

INFORMATION
The mixture is made up of two solids.
The mixture contains one ingredient that is about the size of a pebble.
The mixture contains one ingredient that is similar in size to particles of salt.
Neither ingredient in the mixture is made from metal.

What might the unidentified mixture be?

a. Iron filings and sugar cubes
b. Grapes and cherries
c. Water and pepper
d. Marbles and sand

10. Students are planning a science experiment to answer a question asked by their teacher. They will release a small toy car down an inclined plane. The students complete their first trial and record how long it takes the toy car to reach the bottom of the inclined plane. For the second trial, the students raise the plane by one level to increase its incline and then record how long it takes the car to reach the bottom. The experiment is done two more times, raising the inclined plane one level higher each time.

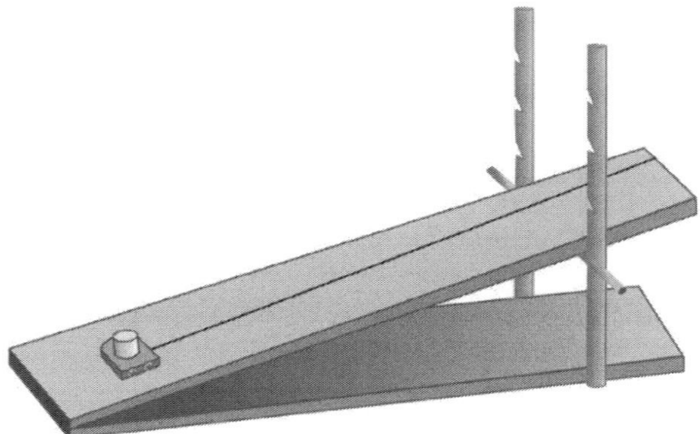

What question are the students most likely trying to answer with this experiment?

a. How can the speed of the car be increased without applying another force?
b. Does the weight of the car affect how fast it can travel?
c. Do different sized cars take different amounts of time to move?
d. How much force does it take to make a toy car move?

11. Identify two statements below that describe a learned behavior. Select all that apply.

a. The child rides a bicycle without training wheels.
b. The fish breathes underwater.
c. A baby cries when upset or hungry.
d. The dog sits down at its food bowl before its owner pours the food.
e. The skunk has a stripe down its back.

12. After studying the water cycle, students were asked to fill in the missing parts of the table below.

Water Cycle Term	Explanation
___1___	The process in which liquid is heated by the Sun and turns into vapor (a gas)
Condensation	The process in which the vapor in the air is __2__ and turns into tiny droplets of water
___3___	The process in which water falls to the surface of the Earth either as a liquid or solid
Collection	The process in which fallen precipitation flows __4__ and collects in rivers, lakes, and oceans

Which shows the correct terms for each missing part?

a. 1. Precipitation
   2. Cooled
   3. Evaporation
   4. Uphill

b. 1. Evaporation
   2. Heated
   3. Cementation
   4. Downhill

c. 1. Evaporation
   2. Cooled
   3. Precipitation
   4. Uphill

d. 1. Evaporation
   2. Cooled
   3. Precipitation
   4. downhill

13. Based on the weather forecast, what can a farmer expect to happen to his bird bath overnight?

10pm	11pm	12am	1am	2am	3am	4am	5am
34°F	33°F	28°F	26°F	24°F	22°F	22°F	21°F

a. Freeze
b. Evaporate
c. Melt
d. Overflow

14. A fifth-grade science student completed a lab that required mixing 15 grams of salt into 500 milliliters of water. The student wrote the following observations in her lab journal.

1. Water is a liquid and takes the shape of its container.
2. Salt is no longer present once it is mixed into the water.
3. The mass of the salt does not change throughout the entire experiment.
4. Salt dissolved in water is an example of a solution.

Which observation is incorrect?

a. Observation 1
b. Observation 2
c. Observation 3
d. Observation 4

15. What is the main way that water from the ocean becomes incorporated into the water cycle?

a. Warm water currents heat up until the water within them evaporates.
b. The Sun heats the water on the surface of the ocean until it evaporates.
c. The thermal energy from marine life heats the water until it evaporates.
d. Underwater volcanoes erupt and cause the water above to evaporate.

16. Which two examples below describe a learned behavior of a squirrel? Select all that apply.

a. The squirrel flicks its tail to warn other squirrels of approaching danger.
b. The squirrel climbs the tree quickly.
c. The squirrel runs under the picnic table at the park to look for dropped food.
d. The squirrel runs in a zigzag pattern to escape a predator.
e. The squirrel waits until a human crosses the street before it runs across the street.

17. The cactus below commonly grows in desert environments because it needs little water and lots of sun to survive.

Which of the characteristics of the cactus listed below is NOT an example of an inherited trait?

a. The cactus has large thorns.
b. The cactus has large, bright flowers.
c. One pad on the cactus is broken off.
d. The cactus needs little water to survive.

18. Which statement best describes what physical change will happen when a barista at a coffee shop stirs sugar into a large, hot coffee?

a. The sugar is less dense than the coffee and floats to the top of the cup.
b. The sugar is soluble and dissolves in the hot coffee.
c. The sugar evaporates from the cup because of the heat.
d. The mass of the sugar decreases.

19. The students are learning the differences between weather and climate. Read each statement below and determine if the statement refers to weather or climate. In the blank next to each statement, write which of the two options it refers to. Choose ONE option for each statement. Each option will be used more than once.

Climate	Weather

1. The temperature outside is 72 degrees Fahrenheit. ____________
2. There are no clouds in the sky today. ____________
3. The average temperature in the spring for the last 50 years in Texas is 72 degrees 4. Last week it snowed three inches each day. ____________
4. Last week it snowed three inches each day. ____________
5. Since 1980, the average amount of rain each year in Idaho is 42 inches. ____________
6. In April, we had more rainy days than sunny days. ____________

20. Students are asked to sort a list of behaviors into two groups: learned and inherited. Which chart below correctly sorts the behaviors?

a.

Learned	Inherited
The toddler chews with his mouth closed.	Some species of birds choose to fly south each winter.
A pet parrot barks like the dog that is also in the home.	The child has freckles all over her face.
The dog runs to the door when it hears the car come up the driveway.	The dog barks, and the cat meows.
The cat runs to its bowl when it hears the cabinet door squeak open.	The sea turtle buries its eggs on the sandy beach.

b.

Learned	Inherited
The toddler chews with his mouth closed.	Some species of birds choose to fly south each winter.
The sea turtle buries its eggs on the sandy beach.	The child has freckles all over her face.
The dog runs to the door when it hears the car come up the driveway.	The dog barks, and the cat meows.
The cat runs to its bowl when it hears the cabinet door squeak open.	A pet parrot barks like the dog that is also in the home.

c.

Learned	Inherited
The toddler chews with his mouth closed.	Some species of birds choose to fly south each winter.
A pet parrot barks like the dog that is also in the home.	The child has freckles all over her face.
The dog barks, and the cat meows.	The dog runs to the door when it hears the car come up the driveway.
The sea turtle buries its eggs on the sandy beach.	The cat runs to its bowl when it hears the cabinet door squeak open.

d.

Learned	Inherited
Some species of birds choose to fly south each winter.	The toddler chews with his mouth closed.
The child has freckles all over her face.	A pet parrot barks like the dog that is also in the home.
The dog barks, and the cat meows.	The dog runs to the door when it hears the car come up the driveway.
The sea turtle buries its eggs on the sandy beach.	The cat runs to its bowl when it hears the cabinet door squeak open.

21. Unlike many creatures, these animals have special types of feet to help them better survive in their environment.

These animals' feet help them survive in what type of environment, and how do they help them survive in that environment?

a. Icy - The animals' webbed feet help them walk across icy surfaces instead of sliding on them.
b. Desert - The animals' webbed feet help them walk across dry sand instead of sinking into it.
c. Mountainous - The animals' webbed feet help them hold onto steep surfaces like mountain faces.
d. Aquatic - The animals' webbed feet help them swim through bodies of water.

22. Students are completing a science lab involving mixtures. They are asked to follow the steps given.

Step 1	Measure $\frac{1}{2}$ cup of sand and place in a mason jar.
Step 2	Measure $\frac{1}{2}$ of sugar and place in the same mason jar.
Step 3	Shake the mason jar vigorously to ensure the sand and sugar are mixed well.
Step 4	Remove the sand from the mixture.

What would be the best way for the students to complete step 4?

a. The students should pour the mixture out on a plate then hold a strong magnet over the plate and move it around. The sand will collect on the magnet.
b. The students should use very small tweezers to carefully remove the sand particles from the sugar particles.
c. The students should slowly pour the mixture through a kitchen strainer. The sugar will collect in the strainer, and the sand will fall through the strainer.
d. The students should pour water into the jar with the mixture and stir until the sugar dissolves. Then, they should pour the contents of the jar through a coffee filter. The sand will remain in the filter, and the sugar water will drain through it.

23. This picture shows a college baseball player hitting a baseball with a baseball bat.

Which choice below correctly shows how the position of the ball will change and gives the correct reason for this change?

a.

The force of gravity forces the ball to fall.

c.

The force of the bat pushes the ball away from the batter.

b.

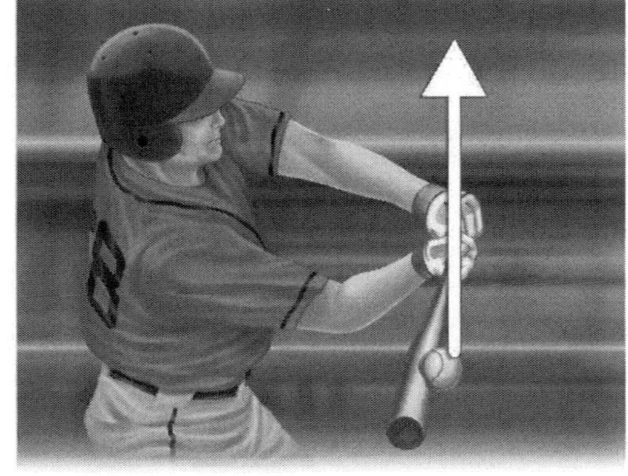

The force of the bat will pull the ball straight up.

d.

The force of the bat pulls the ball away from the batter.

24. Students were asked to match the environment description to an animal that would be supported in that ecosystem. Below are the answers from one student.

ENVIRONMENT	ANIMAL
Icy water with freezing temperatures most of the year	________
Swampy area with warm temperatures	________
Hot, beachy area near the ocean	________
Warm, rocky grasslands and plains	________

Match the correct animals with the environments described. Not all answer choices will be used.

Polar bear	Crab	Alligator
Panda bear	Lion	Shark

25. A grassland food chain is shown below.

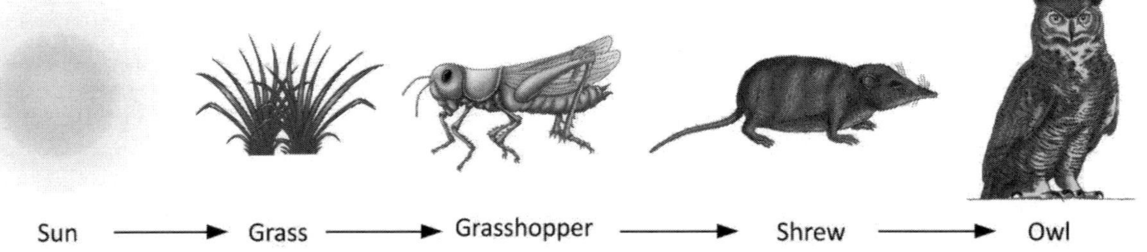

What is the producer in this food chain, and where does it receive its energy?

a. The owl is the producer, and it receives its energy from the Sun.
b. The shrew is the producer, and it receives its energy from the grasshopper.
c. The grasshopper is the producer, and it receives its energy from the grass.
d. The grass is the producer, and it receives its energy from the Sun.

26. Which correctly matches the body organ with its function?

a. Liver: helps to move blood throughout the body
b. Small intestines: absorbs nutrients from food
c. Heart: aids in breathing
d. Diaphragm: allows the body to move

27. Students were asked to write a sentence explaining where most of the water that is evaporated in our world comes from. Which student wrote the correct explanation?

a. Most of the evaporated water in the world comes from the oceans because the oceans are the largest source of water in our world.
b. Lakes are the largest source for water evaporation because it is fresh water.
c. Water is mostly evaporated from creeks because the moving water in creeks allows evaporation to happen more quickly.
d. Ponds are responsible for most of the evaporation in our world because the creatures that live in the pond add warmth, which speeds up evaporation.

28. The science teacher showed a video of a baseball in motion. What change must occur to an object for it to be in motion?

a. A mass change must occur for an object to be in motion.
b. A position change must occur for an object to be in motion.
c. A frictional change must occur for an object to be in motion.
d. A gravitational change must occur for an object to be in motion.

29. Students were asked to write about a chemical change that occurred due to a temperature change. Which student wrote the correct response?

a. Student 1: Dew formed on the morning grass when the water vapor in the air was heated by the sun.
b. Student 2: The copper bowl was hammered with a small, heated mallet to add texture and design to the bowl.
c. Student 3: The metal nails on the deck began to rust after several months of exposure to cold snow.
d. Student 4: The log turned to ash when it was burned in the fireplace.

30. Stella wants to create a model to illustrate how condensation works as part of the water cycle. Which of the following models would work best to illustrate this concept?

a. Stella could put a pot of water on a hot plate to illustrate how when water is heated, it turns to water vapor.
b. Stella could show the students the water particles that are formed on the outside of a glass of ice to illustrate how water vapor is cooled.
c. Stella could use an eye dropper to drop tiny drops of water into a tray to show how the water combines quickly.
d. Stella could put a heat lamp over a tank of water to show how water vapor is formed.

31. The human body sends signals to initiate movement or to warn of dangers. Which pair of organs below work closely together to send these signals?

a. Brain and spinal cord
b. Lungs and stomach
c. Heart and bladder
d. Eyes and pancreas

32. The science teacher asked the students to use the map below to write a comparison statement about the expected temperatures of two of the numbered areas below.

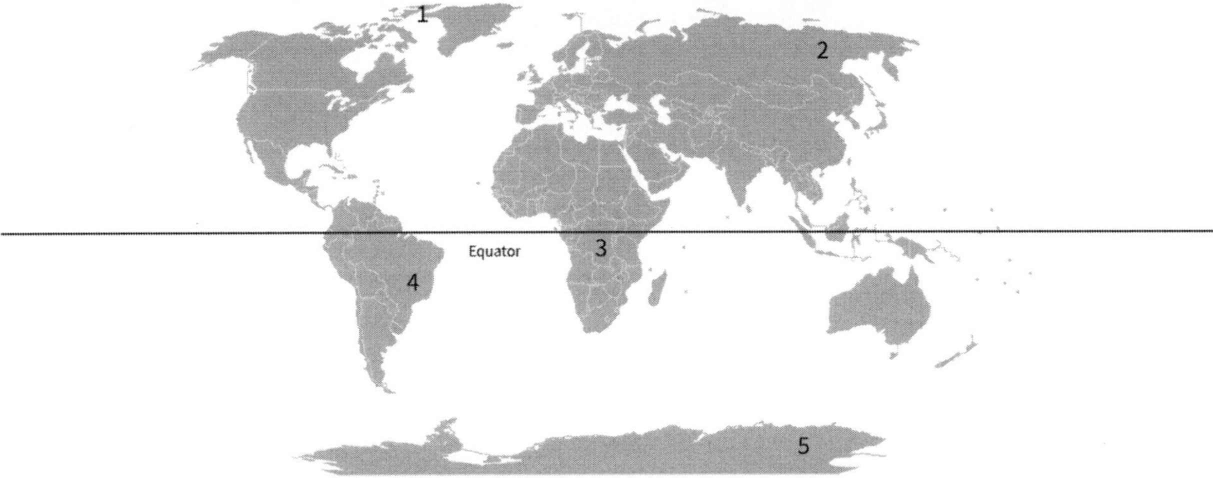

Which student wrote a statement that correctly compared the temperatures of two of the numbered areas on the map?

a. Student 1: Areas 2 and 5 would most likely have very similar temperatures throughout the year since they are both located in the eastern hemisphere of the world.
b. Student 2: Areas 3 and 4 would most likely have very different temperatures throughout the year since they are on different continents.
c. Student 3: Areas 1 and 4 would most likely have very similar temperatures throughout the year because they are both located near large bodies of water.
d. Student 4: Areas 1 and 3 would most likely have very different temperatures throughout the year because area 3 is right at the equator and area 1 is very far from the equator.

33. Which of the following situations would produce the greatest change in motion?

a. The quarterback threw the regulation football using 50 Newtons of force.
b. The field goal kicker kicked the regulation football using 62 Newtons of force.
c. The coach tossed the regulation football using 21 Newtons of force.
d. The punter kicked the regulation football using 66 Newtons of force.

34. Students were asked to write one fact about the food chain shown below.

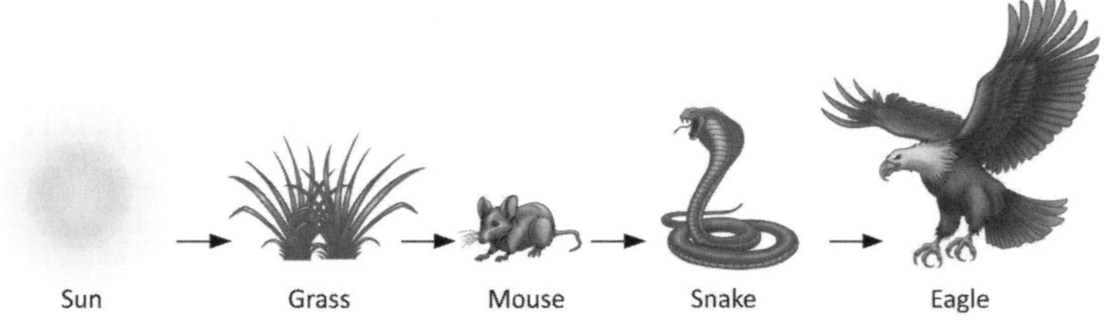

Which statement about the food chain is NOT correct?

a. Energy is transferred from the snake to the eagle.
b. The sun's energy is transferred to the grass.
c. The grass is a consumer.
d. The mouse provides energy for the snake.

35. Apple trees grow well in the moist environment of northern Florida.

The bark on the apple tree has a similar function to what human organ?

a. Lungs
b. Skin
c. Brain
d. Large intestine

36. Students in Mrs. Peterson's class recorded different weather conditions in three different areas. Their data is displayed in the table below.

	Area 1	Area 2	Area 3
Temperature	85°F	82°F	90°F
Precipitation	5 cm	2 cm	4 cm
Humidity	85%	50%	60%
Wind	3 mph from the North	4 mph from the West	4 mph from the East

Which statement about the weather is true for all three areas?

a. There are dangerously high winds in all three areas.
b. It will be a snowy day for all three areas.
c. Citizens living in these areas should wear a large coat.
d. The precipitation expected in all three areas will be rain.

37. North Carolina is on the east coast of the United States and meets the Atlantic Ocean. Which statement is true about areas near large bodies of water?

a. Areas near large bodies of water have much colder temperatures than areas further away from water.
b. Areas near large bodies of water receive more rain than areas further away from water.
c. Areas near large bodies of water have warmer temperatures than areas further away from water.
d. Areas near large bodies of water are drier than areas further away from water.

38. Raul and Rebecca were both given a bag of ice. Raul placed his bag of ice under a shade tree, and Rebecca placed her bag of ice in the middle of the track. It was very sunny that day, and when the students returned an hour later, Raul's bag still contained several ice cubes, while Rebecca's bag was now completely water. Why did this happen?

a. The bag of ice heated more quickly in the sun than in the shady area.
b. Students probably stepped on the bag of ice that was on the track.
c. The bag of ice was protected on the track, but not under the shade tree.
d. The bag of ice heated more quickly in the shady area.

39. As a part of a project about the weather differences in various environments, Ashley made the chart below to show the averages for two areas.

	Area 1	Area 2
Temperature	105°F	30°F
Precipitation	0 cm	3 cm snow
Humidity	1%	50%
Wind	0 mph from the South	20 mph from the North

Which could be the areas described in Ashley's chart?

a. Area 1: tropical rainforest, Area 2: Saharan desert
b. Area 1: mountain peak, Area 2: Saharan desert
c. Area 1: tropical rainforest, Area 2: Artic tundra
d. Area 1: Saharan desert, Area 2: mountain peak

40. A student takes the trash can to the curb every Tuesday and Thursday for trash collection. On Tuesday the trash container only had one trash bag inside. On Thursday, the trash container had five trash bags inside. Which statement describes a change that occurred on Thursday?

a. The force needed to move the trash container at the same speed will decrease from Tuesday to Thursday.
b. The force needed to move the trash container at the same speed will remain the same on Tuesday and Thursday.
c. The force needed to move the trash container at the same speed will increase from Tuesday to Thursday.
d. The force needed to move the box at the same speed will decrease and then increase on Thursday.

41. The Florida panther is the most endangered species that currently lives in the everglades of southern Florida. Which of the following has the biggest negative impact on the population of the Florida panther?

a. the increase in population of the snapping turtle
b. human interference such has the building of factories and highways
c. predators such as feral hogs and deer
d. the introduction of different plant species

42. A horse is an example of a ________.

a. parasite
b. producer
c. decomposer
d. consumer

43. In a food chain, where does energy go after the secondary consumer dies?

a. Back to the Sun
b. To the producers
c. Into the air, becoming wind
d. To decomposers

44. Olivia threw each of the items below using the same force of 20 Newtons. Which object traveled the shortest distance?

Object	Pushing Force	Mass	Object
Bouncy Ball	20 Newtons	38 grams	Bouncy Ball
Baseball	20 Newtons	145 grams	Baseball
Tennis Ball	20 Newtons	57.7 grams	Tennis Ball
Golf Ball	20 Newtons	45.9 grams	Golf Ball

a. Bouncy ball
b. Baseball
c. Tennis ball
d. Golf ball

45. Which trait of a child is NOT an inherited trait?

a. The child is tall and has brown hair like his father.
b. The child is color blind like her mom and dad.
c. The child speaks Spanish like her mother.
d. The child has many freckles on her face like her dad.

46. The trunk and bark of the live oak tree has a similar function to which part of another organism?

a. the gills of a sailfish
b. the exoskeleton of an apple snail
c. the feathers of a blue heron
d. the claws of the black bear

47. The following represents a simple food chain. What trophic level contains the greatest amount of energy?

tree → caterpillar → frog → snake → hawk → worm

a. tree
b. caterpillar
c. hawk
d. worm

48. Students measured the weather conditions on Monday using a thermometer to measure temperature and an anemometer to measure wind speed. The readings on the weather tools are shown below.

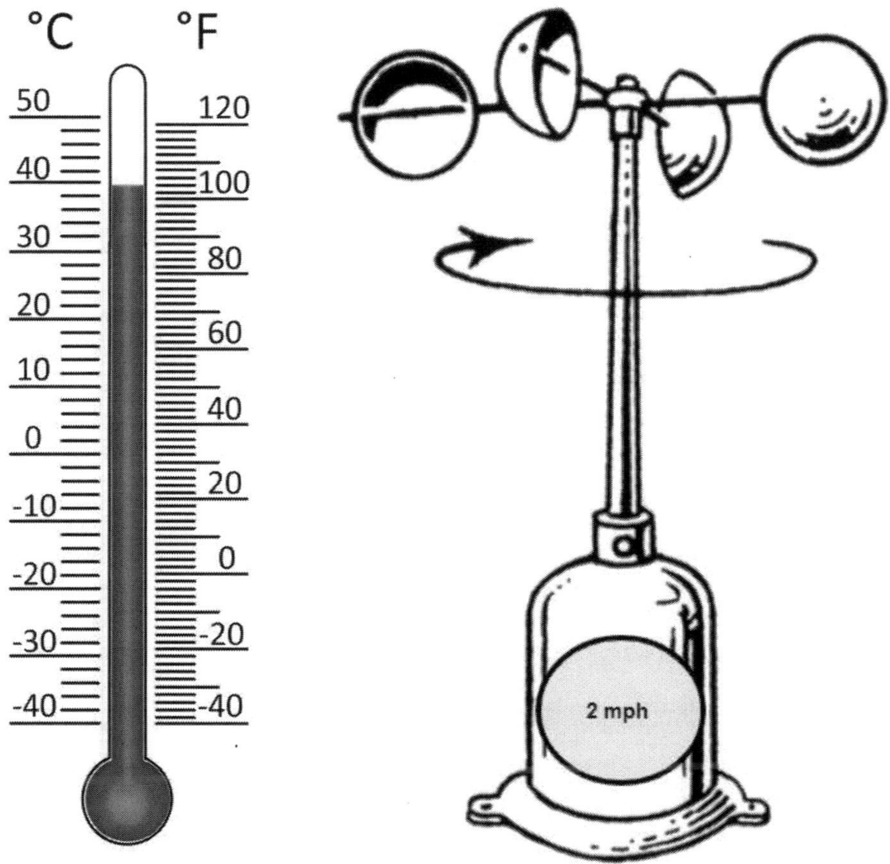

Based on these readings, which best describes the weather on Monday?

a. Windy and rainy
b. Cold and windy
c. Hot and not windy
d. Snowy and not windy

49. Students were asked to write a paragraph about a time they saw energy creating a change during a sporting event. The students submitted the following topics to the teacher. Which topic does NOT illustrate energy creating a change?

> **Topic 1:** The baseball soared into right field after the batter hit it with the bat.
> **Topic 2:** The player threw the basketball up to the hoop, but it rolled off the rim.
> **Topic 3:** The soccer ball sat in the middle of the field before the game started.
> **Topic 4:** The football flew straight threw the middle of the goal post after the player kicked it.

a. Topic 1
b. Topic 2
c. Topic 3
d. Topic 4

50. Many organisms such as crabs and shrimp can be found in the Atlantic Ocean along the east coast of North Carolina. Which other organism can be found in the Atlantic Ocean?

a. eagle
b. lobster
c. monkey
d. alligator

51. A student owns a poodle and makes a list of its characteristics to find its inherited and acquired physical traits. Which of the following questions would help the student understand which of the poodle's traits is acquired?

Has four legs Has a fluffy tail Has one eye Has white fur

a. How many legs do the poodle's parents have?
b. What color is the poodle's fur in winter?
c. Did the poodle have one eye when the family adopted it?
d. Was the poodle born with a fluffy tail?

52. Which of the following is NOT true for all cells?

a. All eukaryotic cells have a nucleus.
b. Cells can only reproduce from existing cells.
c. Cells are the basic structures of any organism.
d. All cells have chloroplast.

Answers and Explanations for Test #1

1. A: Plants are considered producers because they are able to absorb light energy from the Sun and convert it into food through the process of photosynthesis. In other words, plants are producers because they produce their own food from sunlight.

2. D: The molecules that make up gases are far apart and move about very quickly. Because they have a weak attraction to each other, they expand to take up as much space as possible.

3. C: The ball will move forwards. The ball is moving forward with the boat. When the front of the boat hits the dock, the ball's motion does not change. It continues to move forward because the force acting to stop the boat is not acting upon the ball. The forward motion of the boat is halted by the dock. The forward motion of the ball is not stopped. Since the ball is round there is little friction to provide an equal and opposite reaction to the forward motion.

4. D: A desert is classified by the average amount of precipitation the region receives on a yearly basis. The temperature is irrelevant, as there are both hot and cold deserts. Due to the dry conditions, only organisms designed to withstand the arid conditions can survive in these areas.

5. D: After a secondary consumer dies, such as a wolf, its body is partially consumed by decomposers, such as bacteria and fungi. Bacteria and fungi live in soil and digest body tissues of dead organisms converting them into basic nutrients that plants need to grow. Therefore, after secondary consumers die, their energy is consumed by decomposers, who make nutrients available in the soil for producers to use. *Do not confuse nutrients in the soil with energy that producers get from the Sun to make their own food.*

6. A: Many organisms, especially organisms that live in harsh conditions such as deserts or frozen icy areas, have developed specific adaptations that allow them to survive. For example, cacti are able to expand to store large amounts of water, coyotes absorb some water from their food, and snakes can escape the heat by hiding within rocks.

7. A: The picture shows an arrow in front of the box pulling the box forward. If the box were being pushed, the arrow would be behind the box pushing it forward. Gravity pulls downward, not forward.

8. D: Kangaroos live in a dry, wide-open environment where there is little coverage from predators. It is important for kangaroos to be able to hear predators coming from a far distance so they can escape. Their large ears help them to hear subtle sounds of potential predators from far away.

9. D: The mixture of marbles and sand fits all the information given (D). Marbles and sand are both solids and not made of metal. A marble is about the same size as a pebble, and sand is similar in size to particles of salt. Furthermore, a kitchen strainer would easily separate marbles and sand. Iron filings (A) are made of metal. Grapes and cherries (B) are both about the same size, and neither is the same size as particles of salt. Water (C) is a liquid, and the information stated that both ingredients were solid.

10. A: The students are trying to increase the speed of the car without physically pushing it with more force, so they are using an incline plane. Through this experiment, the students should discover that raising the level of the inclined plane increases the speed of the car. The car's weight

(B) and size (C) were never changed, and the exact amount of force was never measured (D). Because of this, these questions could not be answered by the experiment.

11. A, D: Choice A is an example of a learned behavior because someone had to teach the child to do this. It was not something he or she was born being able to do. Choice B and choice C are both examples of inherited traits because those are behaviors the fish and baby know how to do from birth. Choice D is an example of a learned behavior because the owner had to teach the dog to behave in this way. Choice E is an example of an inherited trait because this is something the skunk was born with.

12. D: In the water cycle, evaporation is the process of water being heated by the Sun and turning into vapor, which is a gas. Condensation is the process of water vapor in the air being cooled and turning into tiny droplets of water. If the vapor were heated, it would continue to be vapor. Precipitation is the process of water falling to the surface of the Earth either as a liquid or solid. Collection is the process of fallen precipitation flowing downhill and collecting in rivers, lakes, and oceans. Water does not naturally flow uphill.

13. A: The weather forecast shows that the temperature will drop well below 32°F overnight and stay in the 20s. The freezing point of water is 32°F, which means that the water in the birdbath will freeze overnight after the temperature drops. Choice B is incorrect because the water in the birdbath would need to get very hot in order to evaporate, which will not happen, according to the forecast. Choice C is incorrect because the water in the birdbath would need to be frozen and then heated in order to melt. Choice D is incorrect because as the water in the birdbath freezes, it will contract and it will appear that there is less than there was. This will not cause the birdbath to overflow.

14. B: Observation 2 (B) is incorrect. Salt is still present in the water. It has dissolved, so it is not clearly visible, but it is still in the water. Observation 1 (A) is correct: water is a liquid and takes the shape of its container. Observation 3 (C) is correct: when a substance is added to a liquid, the mass of the substance does not change. Observation 4 (D) is correct: dissolving salt in water is an example of creating a solution.

15. B: The Sun shines down and heats the water on the surface of the oceans. This causes ocean water to evaporate and follow the steps of the water cycle. Water in warm water currents does not get hot enough to evaporate, so choice A is incorrect. Animals that live in the ocean cannot produce enough heat to cause water to evaporate, so choice C is incorrect. While underwater volcanoes may erupt and drastically heat up water, this is not the way that most water vapor from the ocean is created. Choice D is incorrect.

16. C, E: The squirrel would have learned over time that there are often leftover bits of food under the picnic table at the park (C). This is not something it was born knowing but instead learned after finding bits of food under the table multiple times. Squirrels learn by watching others, and they have learned to wait to cross the street until humans do (E). Since squirrels have learned this over time, it is a learned behavior. The squirrel instinctively knows to flick its tail (A), climb (B), and run in a zigzag pattern (D).

17. C: A pad on the cactus being broken off is a result of an interaction with an outside source. It is not an example of something inherited. A cactus does inherit its thorns (A), flowers (B), color, and need for little water (D).

18. B: A physical change will occur when the sugar dissolves in the coffee. Sugar is soluble in liquids like coffee (B). Sugar is denser than coffee, not less (A), but either way, this does not describe a physical change. Sugar will not evaporate from the coffee cup (C). When a substance dissolves in a liquid, the mass of the substance does not change (D).

19.

Climate	Weather
1. The temperature outside is 72 degrees Fahrenheit.	Weather
2. There are no clouds in the sky today.	Weather
3. The average temperature in the spring for the last 50 years in Texas is 72 degrees 4. Last week it snowed three inches each day.	Climate
4. Last week it snowed three inches each day.	Weather
5. Since 1980, the average amount of rain each year in Idaho is 42 inches.	Climate
6. In April, we had more rainy days than sunny days.	Weather

20. A: The toddler doesn't automatically chew with his mouth closed. He is taught by a parent to do this, so it is a learned behavior. A parrot is not born with the desire to bark like a dog. The parrot learned this sound from the other family pet. The dog has learned that when the car comes up the driveway, its owner is home and about to come in the door. It has learned to run to the door to greet its owner. The cat runs to its bowl when the squeaky cabinet opens because through repetition the cat has learned that after this sound, it usually gets fed. Birds flying south for the winter, cats meowing, dogs barking, and sea turtles burying their eggs on the beach are all examples of inherited behaviors. These animals were not taught to do these things but know to do them naturally. The child inherited the freckles from someone in her family.

21. D: The webbed feet on these animals help them travel through an aquatic environment quickly and efficiently. Webbed feet are common in animals that live near water. They help animals swim through the water quickly by making their feet more like paddles and also allow animals to walk on land. Webbed feet might help an animal walk across sand, but they are not best suited to areas with lots of dry sand, like the desert (B). Though many aquatic environments include wet and dry sand, webbed feet make animals better suited to traveling through the water, not the sand. Webbed feet would not help an animal hold onto a steep surface (C). In fact, they would make it more difficult for an animal to crawl up a steep surface or walk on the rocky, uneven ground found in the mountains. Since webbed feet are often flat and smooth, they do not prevent animals from sliding on ice (A). However, some animals that live in icy places, such as penguins, have webbed feet. Many penguins have webbed feet with small claws that allow them to swim and walk across ice easily.

22. D: Since sugar is soluble in water, the sugar in the mixture will dissolve, leaving sand and sugar water. When poured through a coffee filter, the sugar water will move through, and the sand will collect in the filter (D). This means it will be separate from the sugar. Neither sand nor sugar is magnetic (A), so a magnet would not be a good way to separate the sand. It would be too difficult and time-consuming to separate the sand using tweezers because of the small size of the sand and sugar pieces (B). Both the sand and sugar would easily move through a kitchen strainer, so option C would not result in the sand being separated.

23. C: When the bat makes contact with the ball, the bat will push the ball forward and away from the batter. The bat provides the force that interacts with the ball, and the force the bat uses is a push (D). The force of gravity will eventually pull the ball to the ground (A). However, because the ball was thrown using a force that sends it in a different direction, it takes longer for gravity to pull it down. Additionally, the bat changes the direction of the ball using another force, so it takes even more time for gravity to pull the ball to the ground. The ball would not go straight up (B) or straight down because the push of the bat forces the ball to move straight forward.

24.

ENVIRONMENT	ANIMAL
Icy water with freezing temperatures most of the year	Polar bear
Swampy area with warm temperatures	Alligator
Hot, beachy area near the ocean	Crab
Warm, rocky grasslands and plains	Lion

A panda bear lives in a cool, rainy forest with lots of access to bamboo. A shark lives in the ocean since it needs salt water to survive. A polar bear needs an environment with icy water and very cold temperatures. An alligator thrives in swampy areas with warm temperatures. A crab can live in the hot sand along the shore. A lion lives in rocky plains and grasslands with warm temperatures.

25. D: The grass is the producer because it makes its own food and does not rely on another organism for its nutrients. The grass receives energy from the Sun that allows it to make its own food. The grasshopper, shrew, and owl are examples of consumers because they need other organisms for food.

26. B: The small intestine is where nutrients are absorbed. The liver breaks down food, the heart pumps blood, and the diaphragm allows for air to enter and exit the lungs.

27. A: Since the oceans are the largest source of water in our world, most evaporation occurs from the ocean. Fresh water does evaporate slightly faster than salt water, but lakes do not provide nearly the amount of water to be evaporated as the oceans do. Running water in creeks and higher temperatures in ponds will also aid in evaporation, but the amount of water in the sources is much smaller than the amount of water in oceans.

28. B: An object like a baseball is in motion when there is a change in the object's position. A mass change would not indicate that an object moved. A frictional change or a gravitational change would affect the motion of an object, but neither is required for an object to be considered in motion.

29. D: Student 4 is correct because a chemical reaction occurred when the log turned to ash. This chemical change occurred when heat from the fire was added to the log. Student 1 is incorrect because morning dew is an example of a physical change and occurs when water vapor in the air is cooled. Student 2 is incorrect because hammering a bowl with a heated mallet is an example of a physical change. Student 3 is incorrect because water from the snow caused the chemical change that formed the rust, not the cold temperature of the snow.

30. B: Water droplets forming on the side of an icy cup perfectly illustrate the process of condensation as the icy cup cools the water vapor in the air and turns that water vapor back into small drops of liquid water. Heating a pot of water with a hot pot or heating a tank of water with a heat lamp would model the process of evaporation. Dropping small drops of water into a tray would model precipitation and collection.

31. A: The spinal cord is the pathway where messages are sent to and from the brain in the human body. These organs work together to send and receive signals to and from various parts of the body.

One would not work without the other. The lungs are responsible for breathing, and the stomach is apart of digestion. The heart pumps blood while the bladder holds urine. The eyes aid in sight, and the pancreas makes digestive fluids.

32. D: Areas located close to the equator have much warmer temperatures than areas that are far away from the equator. Area 3 is located along the equator so temperatures in that location are very warm. Area 1 is located far north of the equator and would therefore have cold temperatures. Being in the same hemisphere does not mean that areas will have similar temperatures. Areas on different continents can have similar temperatures if the areas are both located relatively the same distance from the equator. Being close to large bodies of water does not mean the areas would have similar temperatures.

33. D: The greatest change in motion of the football would occur when the most force is applied to the regulation football, which in this example was 66 Newtons of force. Less force is applied to the football in all of the other options and would result in a smaller change in motion.

34. C: The grass is a producer because it makes its own food using energy from the sun. It is not a consumer because it does not consume an organism to gain energy. The snake provides energy to the eagle when the eagle consumes the snake. The sun is what gives the grass energy to make its own food. The mouse provides energy for the snake when it is consumed by the snake.

35. B: The bark on an apple tree provides protection to the tree like the way the skin provides protection to the human body. The lungs are responsible for respiration, the brain sends signals throughout the body, and the large intestine aids digestion.

36. D: Rain would be the expected precipitation since the temperatures in all three areas are very warm. The wind speed for all the areas is very low, so the winds would not be dangerous. The temperatures are all very warm, so citizens would not need to wear coats and snow would not be possible with the temperatures well above freezing.

37. B: Areas near large bodies of water receive more rainfall than areas further away from water. The large bodies of water add a lot of moisture to the air which results in more rainfall. Areas near water can have warmer or colder climates depending on their distance from the equator. Areas near water are wetter, not drier, than other areas.

38. A: The bag of ice melted on the track because it received radiant energy from the Sun and was heated more quickly than the bag of ice that was in the shade and therefore not receiving direct radiant energy. Human interaction was not the cause of the ice melting and not melting. The bag of ice was not protected on the track. The ice heated more quickly on the track, not in the shady area.

39. D: Area 1 is very hot with little rainfall. This type of weather is consistent with a desert environment, such as the Saharan desert. Area 2 is cold with snow. This type of weather is consistent with a mountain peak because of its higher altitude. A tropical rainforest would receive rain, and Area 1 did not. The temperatures in Area 2 are too cold for a Saharan desert. Area 1 is too warm for a mountain peak or Arctic tundra. Snow would not be expected in a tropical rainforest.

40. C: The mass of the trash container increased as more trash bags were added so more force will be needed to move the trash container at the same speed. The force needed to move the trash container will not decrease or remain the same because more trash bags were in the container, giving it a greater mass.

41. B: Humans have had the biggest negative impact on the Florida panther population in the everglades as more factories and highways have been built taking away the habitat for the Florida panther. The snapping turtle and Florida panther do not share similar habitats. Feral hogs and deer are the prey of the Florida panthers, not predators. Different plant species have little effect on the Florida panther.

42. D: Horses eat plants which are producers. Therefore, horses are consumers.

43. D: After a secondary consumer dies, such as a wolf, its body is partially consumed by decomposers, such as bacteria and fungi. Bacteria and fungi live in soil and digest body tissues of dead organisms, converting them into basic nutrients that plants need to grow. Therefore, after secondary consumers die, their energy is consumed by decomposers, who make nutrients available in the soil for producers to use. *Do not confuse nutrients in the soil with energy that producers get from the Sun to make their own food.*

44. B: The baseball would travel the smallest distance. The greater the mass of the object, the less effect the force will have on the object, causing it not to travel as far as something with less mass. The bouncy ball, tennis ball, and golf ball would travel a greater distance with the same force because of their smaller amount of mass.

45. C: Speaking Spanish is a skill that is not genetic or inherited, as it is learned. Height, hair color, freckles, and color blindness are all genetic traits children can inherit from their parents.

46. B: The exoskeleton of an apple snail protects the snail's inner organs like the bark protects the inner parts of the live oak tree. The gills of the sailfish help the fish to breathe in water, the feathers help the blue heron fly, and the claws of the black bear assist in killing prey.

47. A: In the food chain of tree → caterpillar → frog → snake → hawk → worm, the tree is at the trophic level with the greatest amount of energy. Trophic level refers to the position of an organism in a food chain. Energy is lost according to the laws of thermodynamics as one moves up the food chain because it is converted to heat when consumers consume. Primary producers, such as autotrophs, are organisms who are at the base and capture solar energy. Primary consumers are herbivores that feed on the producers. Secondary consumers consume primary consumers and so on. Decomposers get their energy from the consumption of dead plants and animals.

48. C: The temperature on the thermometer reads over 100 degrees Fahrenheit which means it is a hot day. The anemometer shows the wind only blowing 2 miles per hour which means it is not windy. Neither of these tools measure the rain. The temperature indicates that it is hot, way too warm for snow.

49. C: The soccer ball never changed or moved so it does not illustrate energy creating a change. The baseball bat hit the baseball, the basketball player threw the basketball, and the football player kicked the football which all illustrate energy creating a change in the position of the ball.

50. B: Lobsters are organisms that live in the ocean. Eagles, monkeys, and alligators do not live in the ocean.

51. D: If the poodle was born with a fluffy tail, it is an inherited trait. An inherited trait is one that is present from birth, so if the poodle was born with a fluffy tail, the student can know this is an inherited trait. However, if the dog's fluffy tail was not present when it was born, a groomer or the family likely cut its fur to achieve a fluffy tail shape, making this an acquired trait. Answer choice A is incorrect because, while the number of legs an animal has is typically inherited, there can be genetic mutations or accidents that cause the parents to have a different number of legs than the offspring. Answer choice B is incorrect because knowing what color the poodle's fur is in winter does not tell the student whether this trait is inherited or acquired. It will only tell the student that the fur color changes or not. Answer choice C is incorrect because even if the poodle only had one eye when the student's family adopted it, that does not mean it was born with only one eye, which would make having one eye an inherited trait. The poodle may have been born with two eyes but lost one before the family adopted it.

52. D: Only plant cells have chloroplast. All eukaryotic cells do have a nucleus. Cells can only reproduce from other existing cells. Cells are the basic structures of any organism.

Practice Test #2

1. Why do some cacti have folds in their outer skin?

a. The folds can expand, allowing the cacti to absorb and store water when it rains
b. The folds help protect the cacti from predators
c. The folds allow them to absorb nutrients from the air
d. The folds provide support, allowing the cacti to grow tall

2. Polar bears, seals and walrus' are all arctic animals that have a thick layer of blubber or fat beneath their skin. What purpose does this layer of blubber serve?

a. Protects them from predators
b. Helps to preserve body heat
c. Aids in finding food
d. Prevents them from drowning in water

3. Which statement correctly describes the relationship between plants and animals?

a. Animals breathe in oxygen and plants release oxygen.
b. Animals breathe in carbon dioxide while plants release carbon dioxide.
c. Animals breathe in carbon dioxide while plants breathe out carbon dioxide.
d. Animals get oxygen from plants by eating the plants.

4. Which of the following does not represent a physical change?

a. Salt dissolved in water
b. A spoiling apple
c. Sand dissolved in water
d. Pulverized rock

5. How is force being applied to the box below?

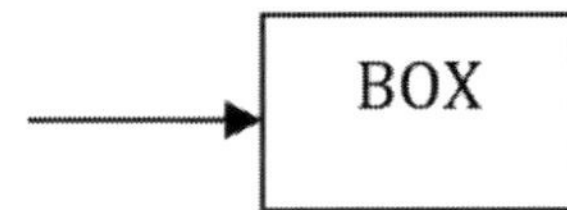

a. The box is being pulled forward
b. The box is being pushed forward
c. Gravity is forcing the box to move forward
d. Friction is forcing the box to stop

6. A Tsunami may be caused by:

a. Earthquakes
b. Volcanoes
c. Landslides
d. A, B, and C

7. Several people were asked to jump on a large trampoline, one at a time, to see who could jump the highest. The results were recorded in the data table below.

Person	Weight	Highest Jump
Sarah	59 kg	1.35 m
Mark	75 kg	1.81 m
Isaac	78 kg	1.93 m
Valerie	64 kg	1.47 m
Crystal	66 kg	1.57 m

Based on the data, what can be concluded about the relationship between weight and jumping height?

a. The more a person weighs, the higher he or she could jump
b. The less a person weighs, the higher he or she could jump
c. A person's weight does not affect how high he or she was able to jump
d. The taller the person is, the higher he or she could jump

8. What does a food chain show?

a. The flow of energy between organisms
b. Every type of species living in a habitat
c. The population of each species in a habitat
d. The number of offspring a species will produce in a year

9. Lions live in savannah and grassland regions where there are tall dry grasses. Lions must sneak up and stalk their prey. What is the most likely reason for a lion's sand colored coat?

a. It allows lions to hide within the grass
b. The light color of their coat reflects heat from the Sun
c. A lion's coloring helps it attract mates
d. It allows them to run faster than their prey

10. An ice cube tray is filled with water. The tray is placed in a freezer for 12 hours. The water freezes forming ice. The tray is removed from the freezer and left on a counter for 12 hours. What changes as the water becomes ice and then melts back into water?

a. The amount of energy in the water
b. The amount of water in the ice cube tray
c. The number of water molecules
d. The mass of the water molecules

11. Why is it more difficult to push a shopping cart full of groceries than an empty shopping cart?

a. The full cart has less mass than the empty cart
b. The full cart has a greater mass than the empty cart
c. The full cart has less friction than the empty cart
d. The empty cart is not pulled down by gravity

12. Algae are part of many food chains. How do algae produce energy?

algae fish seal shark

a. They hunt fish for food
b. Algae undergo photosynthesis
c. They decompose dead or dying organisms
d. They consume fossil fuel from beneath Earth's surface

13. A tropical flower is planted in a local garden. The garden is watered 2 to 3 times per week during all seasons. After only a few months the tropical plant begins to droop and turn brown. How did environmental change most likely affect the tropical plant?

a. Being watered 2 to 3 times per week was not enough to sustain a tropical plant
b. The new environment was too hot and burned the plant
c. Insects attacked the plant causing it to wilt
d. The new soil lacked the nutrients necessary to maintain the plant's health

14. Flowers, trees, and shrubs are all examples of what?

a. Carnivores
b. Herbivores
c. Producers
d. Predators

15. Which picture below shows an example of a learned behavior?

a. 

b. 

c. 

d. 

16. The teacher asked two students to help her move a heavy box to the classroom across the hall in the direction of the arrow.

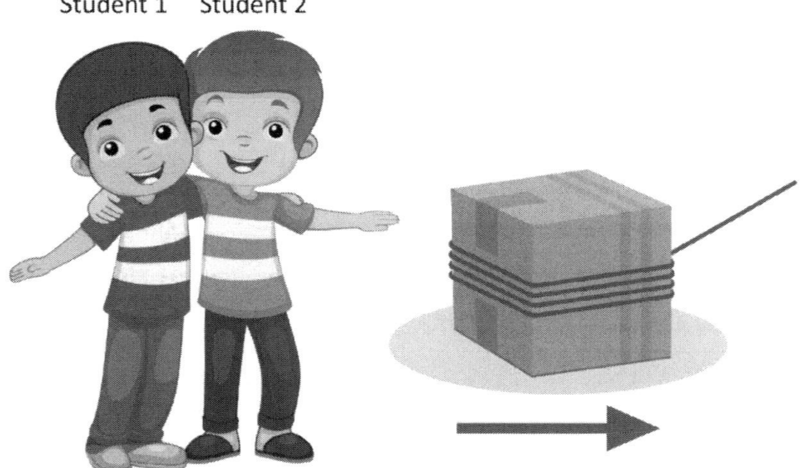

Which of the following describes the easiest way for the students to move the box?

a. Student 1 should take the rope and pull the box in the direction of the arrow. Student 2 should stand on the opposite side of the box and push it in the direction of the arrow.
b. Student 1 should take the rope and pull the box in the opposite direction of the arrow. Student 2 should stand on the same side of the box as student 1 and push the box in the opposite direction of the arrow.
c. Student 1 and student 2 should both stand on the opposite side of the box from the rope and take turns pushing the box in the direction of the arrow.
d. Student 1 should take the rope and pull the box in the direction of the arrow. Student 2 should stand on the opposite side of the box and pull it in the opposite direction of the arrow.

17. The Sun and ocean interact with each other as part of the water cycle. The following chart lists the events in the water cycle.

Water from the ocean condenses into clouds.	Precipitation falls into the ocean.
The Sun evaporates ocean water into the atmosphere.	The Sun warms the ocean water.

What is the correct order of events in how the Sun and ocean in the water cycle? Move one correct answer to each box.

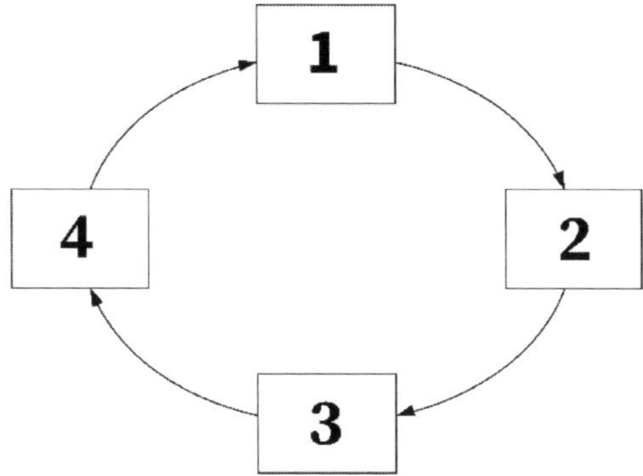

18. Students have been learning about the prickly pear cactus that is often found living in dry, arid locations such as a desert.

Which of the following describes a trait of the prickly pear cactus that protects the plant from predators, and how does that trait protect the cactus?

a. The prickly pear cactus has roots that grow best in sandy soil. The cactus can easily move through sandy soil to escape from predators.
b. The prickly pear cactus has sharp spines that cover its stem and pads. The spines can poke predators and prevent them from eating the cactus.
c. The prickly pear cactus has a thick stem that stores water. The cactus can live in dry conditions that predators cannot survive in.
d. A mature prickly pear cactus has a stem that is strong enough to endure strong wind. The cactus can stay in place during a windstorm, while predators must leave the area.

19. A science teacher prepared five different mixtures for the students to explore. Each mixture contains two to four ingredients, and each mixture has been placed in a separate glass jar. Which two mixtures could easily be separated using magnetism? Select all that apply.

a. Trail mix containing peanuts, raisins, marshmallows, and chocolate chips
b. Sand and small pieces of sea glass
c. Steel bolts and plastic washers
d. Seasoning blend with salt, pepper, and garlic powder
e. Iron filings and sand

20. After a long afternoon of football practice, a fifth grader comes home and decides to make a big bottle of lemonade. The student pours a pouch of powdered lemonade mix into an empty water bottle and then fills the container with cold water. The student shakes the bottle for about one minute. How will the powdered lemonade mix change?

a. The powdered lemonade mix will completely dissolve in the solution.
b. The powdered lemonade mix will disappear and no longer be part of the solution.
c. The powdered lemonade mix will evaporate from the water and no longer be present.
d. The powdered lemonade mix is less dense than the water, so it will float to the top.

21. A student is writing an essay about the different learned behaviors of animals she saw at the aquatic park. She began by writing the outline below.

Learned Behaviors:

- The orca whale jumps out of the water when the trainer raises her hand.
- The seal claps its hands when the trainer claps his hands.
- The dolphin swims straight to the bucket of fish when it is released into the large pool.
- ____________________________________.

Which of the following sentences belongs in the empty place on the outline?

a. The fish in the aquarium have large fins that help them move through the water easily.
b. The sea lion eats the fish that the trainer leaves out for it.
c. The penguins are about 3.5 feet tall.
d. The sea otters roll over on the stage when a whistle is blown.

22. The observations outlined below were made about a pot of water over a campfire. What is the most likely explanation for these observations?

The pot was half full of water The pot hung over the campfire for 15 minutes The water began boiling after 7 minutes A white vapor was observed over the pot After 15 minutes, the pot was one quarter of the way full

a. Some of the water disappeared
b. The water boiled over and some of it spilled out of the pot.
c. Some of the water changed from a liquid to a gas, which was the vapor observed
d. The pot was never half full, someone measured incorrectly

23. The image below illustrates how water droplets sometimes form on the side of a cold glass of water.

In which part of the water cycle pictured below does this process also occur?

a. Number 1
b. Number 2
c. Number 3
d. Number 4

24. The digestive system is responsible for breaking down food in the body. Which correctly illustrates the order food is processed through the organs of the digestive system?

a. Mouth to stomach to intestines to pancreas
b. Mouth to esophagus to intestines to liver
c. Mouth to esophagus to stomach to intestines
d. Mouth to liver to intestines to stomach

25. A student pushes a box around the classroom collecting extra books from classmates' desks. As more books are added to the box, it becomes harder to push. Which of the following would make it easier to move the box?

a. Balance the force by adding a few more books to the box.
b. Decrease the force having one student pull the box while another student pushes the box in the opposite direction.
c. Increase the force by having another student help to push the box in the same direction.
d. Increase the force by increasing the speed at which the box is moving.

26. Move the correct choices from the table to complete the statements.

a push	magnetism	friction	gravity

Vincent and Elizabeth are investigating forces using a kickball. Vincent kicks the ball straight into the air. The force that caused the ball to move up was _________________________. The ball then falls back down onto the ground. The force that caused the ball to move back down was _________________________.

27. The oceans are where much of the Earth's water is collected as a part of the water cycle. The water gets heated by the Sun and evaporates out of the oceans. What term describes the process that allows the oceans to collect more water again?

a. Condensation
b. Precipitation
c. Transportation
d. Transpiration

28. Which statement describes how Earth's relationship to the Sun allows the polar ice caps to remain frozen?

a. The equator receives the most direct sunlight while the poles receive the least amount of sunlight.
b. The Moon reflects the Sun's light away from the North and South Pole preventing them from heating up.
c. Wind currents constantly move air warmed by the Sun away from the North and South Pole and toward the equator.
d. The Sun does not shine on the North or South Pole so they never warm up.

29. The image below shows a popular Atlantic coast plant, sea oats.

Sea oats have tall stems and grow near sand dunes on the beaches of Florida. The sea oats in Florida have adapted to have a large root system that travels deep into the sand. How is the deep and complex root system an adaptation that helps the plant survive on the beaches in Florida?

a. The root system provides stability for the plant in windy conditions and loose sandy soil.
b. The deep root system helps the sea oats receive more freshwater than they would receive with shallow roots.
c. The complex root system helps the sea oats reproduce quickly and increase the population at a rapid rate.
d. The root system keeps humans from easily pulling up or interfering with the growth of the sea oats.

30. Students used a hygrometer to determine the humidity present on several spring days in a coastal area of Florida. They compared their results with the weather reports from a more inland location in Florida. The comparison is shown below.

DAY	HUMIDITY IN INLAND AREA	HUMIDITY IN COASTAL AREA
Monday	57%	75%
Tuesday	63%	82%
Wednesday	52%	79%

Which statement below is NOT true based on the observations in the chart?

a. The highest humidity in both areas occurred on Tuesday.
b. The humidity in the coastal area was greater than the humidity in the inland area.
c. The lowest humidity for both areas occurred on Monday.
d. The humidity during the three days was always the lowest in the inland areas.

31. Two children are fighting over a teddy bear and are pulling on the bear in the direction of the arrows. The force child 1 uses to pull the bear is shown below.

Based on the picture above, which statement about the force and motion of the bear is true?

a. The bear will move in the direction of child 1 if child 2 pulls at a force greater than 20 newtons.
b. The bear will move in the direction of child 1 if the force child 2 uses is equal to the force used by child 1.
c. The bear will not move if child 2 uses a force of exactly 20 newtons when pulling the bear.
d. The bear will move in the direction of child 2 if the force child 2 uses is less than 20 newtons.

32. A student is working on creating a model of the water cycle to present to her science class. The student pours water into half of a five-gallon clear bucket and then places a clear lid on top of the bucket like the picture below.

What could be added to the model to allow evaporation to occur?

a. A bag of ice
b. A container of water
c. A heat lamp
d. A small fan

33. The Florida leafwing has beautiful orange coloring on the inside of its wings that can be seen during flight. However, when the leafwing lands and closes its wings, they are a gray color that resembles the branches in a tree. How does this coloring benefit the Florida leafwing?

a. The orange coloring allows the leafwing to blend in with the flowers in the area.
b. The gray coloring provides camouflage to protect the leafwing from predators when it lands.
c. The coloring changes allow the leafwing to confuse its predator into thinking it is two different creatures.
d. The coloring allows other leafwings to find each other more easily.

34. Blood is moved throughout the body in arteries and veins. What human organ pumps blood so that it can be moved by arteries and veins?

a. Lungs
b. Liver
c. Pancreas
d. Heart

35. Miguel is cooking pasta on the stove. He pours two cups of water in the pot, adds the pasta, places the pot on the stove, and turns it on. After ten minutes, Miguel notices steam rising from the pot. Why is this happening?

a. The pasta at the bottom of the pot was burning, causing smoke to rise from the pot.
b. The water in the pot was heated and is evaporating, causing water vapor to rise from the pot.
c. The heat under the pot is too hot, creating steam.
d. The steam forms as the water cools after the pasta is finished cooking.

36. The baseball player hit the baseball causing it to fly into center field and then fall to the ground. Which correctly describes the force that caused the ball to fall to the ground?

a. The push off the bat
b. The pull of gravity
c. The push of the air
d. The pull of friction

37. Which statement is true about these bolded areas near the equator.

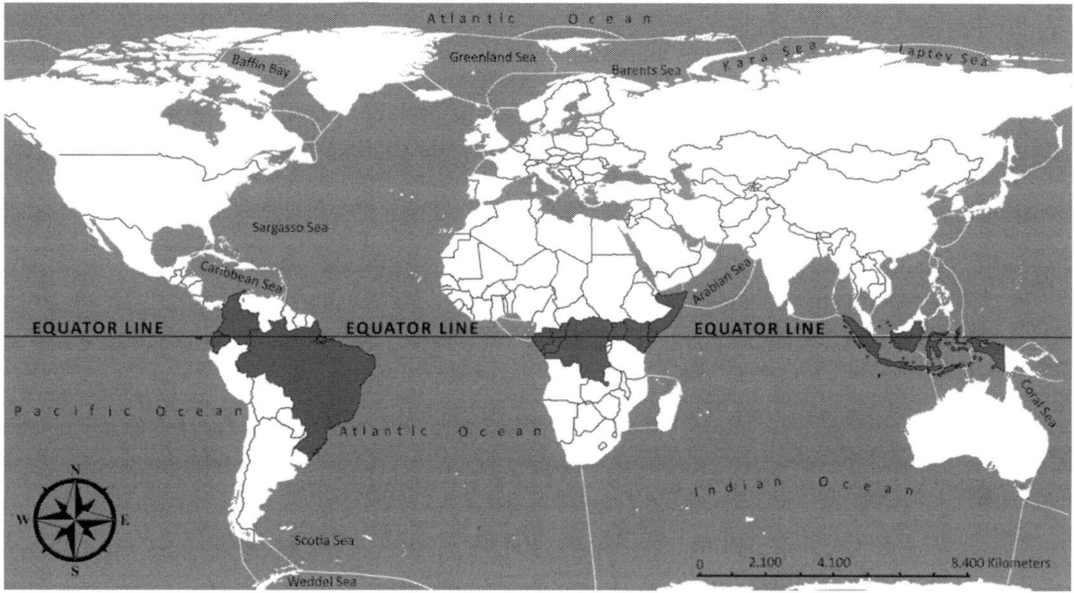

a. These areas receive a high average snowfall each year.
b. These areas are completely surrounded by water.
c. These areas usually have a very warm climate.
d. These areas have a lower temperature when compared to other areas.

38. A diagram of the water cycle is shown below. An important step of the water cycle is labeled with an "X."

What is the main source for this step of the water cycle?

a. Lakes and rivers
b. Melted glaciers
c. Oceans
d. Ponds and lakes

39. Which group of major parts and organs make up the immune system?

a. Lymphatic system, spleen, tonsils, thymus, and bone marrow
b. Brain, spinal cord, and nerve cells
c. Heart, veins, arteries, and capillaries
d. Nose, trachea, bronchial tubes, lungs, alveolus, and diaphragm

40. Which situation does NOT illustrate a situation in which the law of gravity is being overcome?

a. A helicopter taking off from the top of a building.
b. A bird flying from one rooftop to the next.
c. Leaves floated to the forest floor during a fall afternoon.
d. A helium balloon being released to soar high in the sky.

41. The meteorologist informed the citizens of North Carolina that the temperature would remain around 75 degrees Fahrenheit throughout the day, there would be no wind, and it would be partly cloudy. What type of precipitation may be expected on this day?

a. snow
b. sleet
c. hail
d. rain

42. How will the table picture below be expected to move?

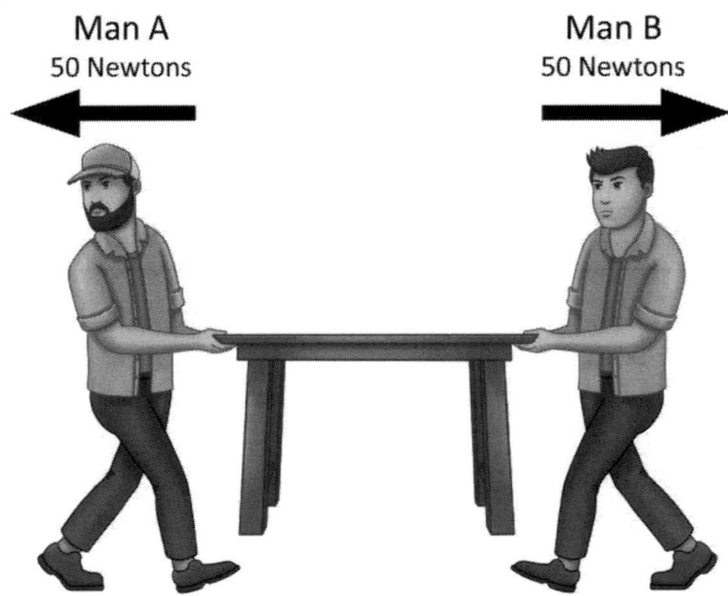

a. The table will move in the direction of Man A because he is pulling in that direction.
b. The table will move in the direction of Man B because he is pulling the table.
c. The table will not move because balanced forces are being applied in opposite directions.
d. The table will fall to the ground because the forces are equal.

43. A man is helping his daughter on the swings in their backyard.

What force will cause the girl to move in the direction of the arrow when the man steps out of the way?

a. The force of friction acting in the direction of the arrow causes the girl to move in the direction of the arrow.
b. The force of gravity acting in the opposite direction of the arrow causes the girl to move in the direction of the arrow.
c. The force of the man pushing his daughter in the opposite direction of the arrow causes the girl to move in the direction of the arrow.
d. The force of gravity pulling the girl toward the Earth causes the girl to move in the direction of the arrow.

44. Identify which statement below describes a learned behavior.

a. The child rides a bicycle without training wheels.
b. The fish breathes underwater.
c. A baby cries when upset or hungry.
d. The skunk has a stripe down its back.

45. A prairie ecosystem is described below. Which organisms from the ecosystem are secondary consumers?

Grass is eaten by grasshoppers, rabbits, and crickets
Corn is eaten by squirrels and beetles
Grasshoppers, beetles, and crickets are all eaten by birds
Squirrels and rabbits are eaten by both foxes and coyotes

a. Corn and grass
b. Grasshoppers and crickets
c. Beetles and squirrels
d. Foxes and coyotes

46. The poisonous dart frog can be bright blue, bright yellow, and even bright orange. Its coloring may be beautiful, but it is used to scare off predators such as snakes. Dart frogs live near moss close to rivers and streams, but sometimes they can be found in tall trees. They like a warm, yet moist environment.

Ecosystem	Temperature Range	Land Features	Plant Life
Q	Very cold winters with lows well below 0 degrees Fahrenheit and mild summers with highs only around 50 degrees Fahrenheit	Glaciers, ice-capped mountains	Spruce trees, sedum
R	Hot summers and warm winters	Sandy dunes	Cactus, agave, brittlebush
S	Mild winters with average temperatures around 45 degrees Fahrenheit and hot summers with highs well above 100 degrees Fahrenheit	Plains and rolling hills	Oak trees, flowers that like full sun
T	Warm and rainy most of the year	Streams and rivers with lush land	Lots of tall trees and vegetation grow at different levels

Which ecosystem described above would be the best for a poison dart frog?

a. Ecosystem Q
b. Ecosystem R
c. Ecosystem S
d. Ecosystem T

47. Students are working in groups to complete an experiment their teacher assigned. The steps for the experiment are listed below.

Experiment Steps
1. Pour $\frac{1}{2}$ cup of hydrogen peroxide into an empty water bottle.
2. Add 1 teaspoon of dish soap to the water bottle.
3. Swirl the water bottle to mix the liquids.
4. In a small glass, mix 1 tablespoon of yeast and 3 tablespoons of warm water.
5. Pour the yeast mixture into the water bottle containing the hydrogen peroxide and dish soap.
6. Place your hand right above the water bottle and notice the heat coming from it.
7. Notice the foam rises in the water bottle and begins to overflow.

Which step above suggests that a chemical reaction occurred during the experiment?

a. Step 2: add 1 teaspoon of dish soap to the water bottle.
b. Step 3: swirl the water bottle to mix the liquids.
c. Step 5: pour the yeast mixture into the water bottle containing the hydrogen peroxide and dish soap.
d. Step 6: place your hand right above the water bottle and notice the heat coming from it.

48. A student makes a list of her characteristics so she can categorize her traits as inherited or acquired physical traits. Which of the following questions would help her understand which of her traits is inherited?

Has brown eyes Has wrinkles Has red hair Has pierced ears

a. Why is the student's hair red?
b. Does the student's friend have brown eyes?
c. Did the student's grandmother have wrinkles?
d. Does the student's mother have her ears pierced?

49. A student is writing an essay about the different learned behaviors of animals she saw at the aquatic park. She began by writing the outline below.

Learned Behaviors:

- The orca whale jumps out of the water when the trainer raises her hand.
- The seal claps its hands when the trainer claps his hands.
- The dolphin swims straight to the bucket of fish when it is released into the large pool.
- ____.

Which of the following sentences belongs in the empty place on the outline?

a. The fish in the aquarium have large fins that help them move through the water easily.
b. The sea lion eats the fish that the trainer leaves out for it.
c. The penguins are about 3.5 feet tall.
d. The sea otters roll over on the stage when a whistle is blown.

50. A student is trying to determine which of her cat's behaviors are instincts and which are learned behaviors. Which TWO of the following questions would help her understand which are learned behaviors?

a. How high was the cat's mother able to jump?
b. Do all cats bring back mice?
c. Did the cat meow since she was a kitten?
d. When did the cat begin to eat treats?

51. A student has made a list of some of the characteristics of the American crow. Which of the following questions could help the student understand which behavior is a learned behavior?

Lives in many places Has dark, glossy feathers Makes tools with found objects Creates a nest

a. At what time of year does the crow make a nest?
b. How do dark, glossy feathers help crows stay hidden?
c. Can crows make tools as soon as they are born?
d. Which color crows live in which places?

52. The meteorologist on television predicted a high temperature of 28 degrees Fahrenheit and at least 5 inches of precipitation. What activity would be most appropriate on this day than the others according to the forecast?

a. Play in the puddles on the sidewalk.
b. Build a snowman.
c. Go to the beach.
d. Go fishing.

Answer Key and Explanations for Test #2

1. A: Cacti live in a desert environment where water is scarce. When it rains, cacti must be able to absorb and store as much water as possible so that they have water available during the dry periods. The folds on the outside of a cactus allow it to expand and fill with water. After a heavy rain, cacti will appear round and plump because the folds are full of water.

2. B: Polar bears, seals, and walrus' all live in arctic climates where it is very cold all year round. The thick layer of blubber that these animals have below the surface of their skin helps them preserve body heat keeping them warm in the frigid environment.

3. A: Animals breathe in oxygen and breathe out carbon dioxide in a process called respiration. Plants use the carbon dioxide that animals exhale, in the process of photosynthesis, and convert it into oxygen.

4. B: A spoiling apple has undergone a chemical change (one substance is changed into another). Dissolving both sand and salt in water, refers to a physical change, since the salt and water and the sand and water can be separated again by evaporating the water, which is a physical change. Pulverized rock is also an example of a physical change where the form has changed but not the substance itself.

5. B: The picture shows an arrow behind the box pushing it forward. If the box were being pulled, the arrow would be in front of the box pulling the box forward. Gravity pulls downward, not forward.

6. D: A tsunami, sometimes referred to as a tidal wave, is a large wave or series of waves caused by the displacement of a large volume of water. While the most common cause is an earthquake, large landslides (either falling into the sea or taking place under water) or explosive volcanic action may also result in a tsunami. Tsunamis take the appearance of very high, sustained tides, and may move water very far inland. Large storms, such as cyclones or hurricanes, may also displace great quantities of water, causing a high tide known as a storm surge that also resembles a tsunami.

7. A: The table shows a clear correlation between mass and jump height. If you put the list of jumpers in order from highest mass to lowest mass, they will also be in order from highest jump height to lowest jump height. Choice D can be eliminated immediately because there is no information about any of the individuals' heights in the data table or in the question.

8. A: A food chain shows how energy flows from one consumer to another. The arrows point in the direction that energy moves. For example, if an arrow points from a flower to a bee, then the energy from the flower flows to the bee as the bee eats the nectar of the flower.

9. A: Lions live in a wide open area where there are few large objects to hide behind. In order to get close enough to their prey to chase and attack it, they must be able to sneak up on it. Their coloration is similar to the color of the tall grasses where they live. This allows the lions to blend into their surroundings and get close to their prey.

10. A: When water changes from a liquid to a solid the amount of thermal energy is decreasing. The molecules move closer together, which creates the solid crystal structure of the ice. As the ice melts back into a liquid, thermal energy level increases, causing the molecules to spread out again.

11. B: The empty shopping cart does not weigh very much and is easy to push. As groceries are added to the empty cart, the cart gains mass. By the time the shopping cart is full, it has more mass than it began with and requires more force to push it.

12. B: Algae are a type of plant that grows in water. Because algae are plants they are able to capture light from the Sun and transform it into energy during the process of photosynthesis.

13. A: Tropical environments typically receive rain 5 to 6 times per week, even if it is only a brief afternoon shower. In its new environment the tropical plant is not receiving enough water to survive.

14. C: Flowers, trees, and shrubs are all plants, which are producers. Producers are able to make their own food using energy from the Sun in a process known as photosynthesis.

15. A polar bear looking after its young (A), a monkey climbing a tree (B), and a spider spinning a web (D) are all examples of inherited behaviors. The organisms were not taught to complete these tasks, but they did them instinctively to survive. However, the dog's behavior is learned since it does not instinctually go retrieve a newspaper (C).

16. A: The greatest force that pushes the box in the direction of the arrow is created when student 1 pulls the rope in the direction of the arrow while student 2 stands on the opposite side of the box and pushes it in the direction of the arrow. In option B, the box would move in the wrong direction. In option C, only one student is pushing at a time, so this would not result in the greatest possible force. In option D, the students are pulling in opposite directions, so the force they create may not send the box in the correct direction.

17.

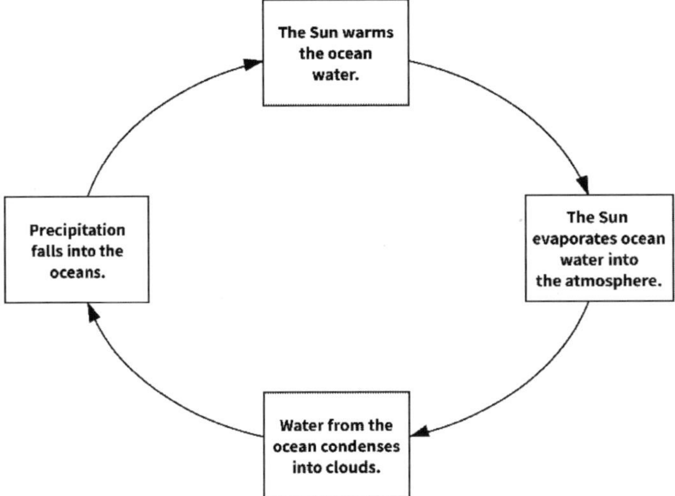

The first step in the water cycle is the Sun warming the ocean. If this did not happen, the amount of water in the atmosphere would not be enough to condense, make clouds, and eventually precipitate. The second step is when the water in the ocean evaporates into the atmosphere due to the heat. As the Sun heats the ocean water, it becomes warm enough to change into a gas. Water vapor then enters the atmosphere. When water vapor enters the atmosphere, it has the tendency to form visible water droplets and condense into clouds, which is the third step of the cycle. Finally, a precipitation event occurs. Rain, hail, snow, or other precipitative weather events occur, and the water re-enters the ocean, starting the cycle again.

18. B: The spines on the prickly pear cactus prevent animals from eating it. The spines do this by poking predators that try to eat the cactus. This impacts how the cactus interacts with biotic factors in its environment. The other traits described affect how the cactus interacts with abiotic factors in its environment. The trait in choice A is related to the type of soil in which the cactus grows, and the roots of the prickly pear cactus do not allow the plant move from one location to another. The trait in choice C is related to the plant's appearance and the amount of water it needs, and there are many herbivores that can also live in the dry conditions that the cactus does. The trait in choice D is related structure and strength of the plant. While it is possible that predators of the prickly pear cactus will have to seek shelter during a windstorm, these organisms can return once the storm is over.

19. C, E: To separate a mixture with a magnet, one of the substances must be magnetic. In option C, the steel bolts are magnetic, so a magnet could be used to pull the steel bolts away from the plastic washers. In option E, the iron filings are magnetic, so a magnet could be used to pull the iron filings away from the sand. Options A, B, and D do not contain any substances that are magnetic, so they are all incorrect.

20. A: A solution occurs when one substance is completely dissolved in a different substance. The powdered lemonade will completely dissolve in the water, creating a solution (A). In a solution, both substances always remain present (C) and part of the solution (B). When mixed, the powdered lemonade will dissolve completely when mixed with the water and will not float to the top (D).

21. D: Someone has taught the otters to roll over each time they hear a whistle. This requires training and is another example of learned behavior. The fish's fin size is an inherited trait of the species (A). Sea lions instinctively eat fish. This statement does not describe the sea lions going to a specific area or performing a trick for the fish. Simply eating the fish is an instinctive behavior (B). The height of the penguins is common for that species and an example of an inherited trait (C).

22. C: Water boils at 100°C. As the pot of water heated up over the campfire, it began to boil. This caused the liquid water to turn into water vapor, a gas. The vapor the campers observed over the boiling pot of water was water vapor. As the water continued to boil, more of the liquid turned into gas, resulting in a decrease in the volume of water in the pot.

23. B: The water droplets form on the glass of ice water as the water vapor in the air is cooled which is called condensation. Condensation is also illustrated at number 2 on the water cycle diagram as the water vapor in the air is cooler and forms water droplets in the clouds. Number one in the water cycle diagram illustrates evaporation, number 3 illustrates precipitation, and number 4 illustrates runoff.

24. C: When digesting food, the food travels from the mouth through the esophagus to the stomach and through the small and large intestines. The liver and pancreas make juices that help to break down food.

25. C: The box would move more easily with an increased force. The force can be increased by adding another student as an additional source of force to push the box in the same direction. The force cannot be increased by increasing the speed. Balancing the forces would cause the box to not move at all, and decreasing the force would make it harder to move the box.

26. A push, gravity: Vincent pushes the ball causing it to move up in the air, and gravity pulls the ball back down to the ground. This example does not illustrate friction slowing down the kickball. Kickballs are not magnetic, and magnetism is not responsible for the movement of the ball.

27. B: Precipitation is responsible for replenishing the water that gets evaporated out of the ocean, and it can come in the form of rain, snow, sleet, or hail. Condensation does not refill the oceans of the Earth, but it is the process in which water vapor is cooled and turned back into small drops of water. Transportation describes movement from one place to the next. Transpiration deals with water evaporating from plant leaves.

28. The equator receives the most direct sunlight while the North and South Pole receive the least amount of direct sunlight. In addition, the atmosphere helps to reflect some of the Sun's heat energy away from the poles. Finally, the reflectivity of the ice helps to deflect some of the heat away from the polar ice caps.

29. A: The windy conditions and loose sandy soil at the beach create an environment where the sea oats could be uprooted easily. The plant has adapted to grow a deep and complex root system to provide stability and keep the plant in the ground. The roots do not provide freshwater for the sea oats since it is near the ocean. The roots are not responsible for reproduction and do not prevent human interference.

30. C: The lowest humidity for the coastal area did occur on Monday, but the lowest humidity for the inland area occurred on Wednesday. This is the statement that is not true. The highest humidity for both areas did occur on Tuesday. The humidity in the coastal area was always greater than the humidity in the inland area and therefore, the humidity in the inland area was always the lowest during the three days.

31. C: Since child 1 is using a force of 20 newtons to pull on the bear, if child 2 uses exactly 20 newtons to pull the other direction on the bear, there will be a balanced force and the bear will not move. If child 2 pulls with a greater force than the 20 newtons child one is using, the bear would move in the direction of child 2. If child 2 pulls with a force less than 20 newtons, the bear would move in the direction of child 1.

32. C: Adding a heat lamp will warm the water and cause evaporation to occur. Adding a bag of ice to the top of the bucket would cool the water vapor in the air, which would create condensation on the lid of the bucket. A container of water would not cause evaporation to occur. A small fan might aid in evaporation in exposed water, but not water in a bucket with a lid.

33. B: The gray coloring on the outside of the leafwing's wings allows it to camouflage itself when landing on tree branches which protects it from predators. The orange is on the inside of the wings so if it lands on a flower, the orange will not be visible. The coloring differences would not confuse a predator nor allow the leafwings to be detected by each other more easily.

34. D: The heart is the organ that pumps blood through the arteries and veins in the human body. The lungs are used for breathing and the liver and pancreas are organs that help humans digest food.

35. B: When the water in the pot was heated, it began to evaporate and can be seen as steam. The steam would not be caused by burnt pasta or overheating. Steam does not form as water cools, but instead as water is heated.

36. B: Gravity is the force that pulled the baseball to the ground. The push of the bat is what sent the baseball flying through the air. The push of the air may cause the ball to go further. There may have been some friction at play, but this would not cause the ball to fall to the ground.

37. C: Areas near the equator have a tropical climate with very warm temperatures. The warmer temperatures do not allow for a high average of snowfall. Although some areas border the ocean, not all the areas are surrounded by water. These areas would have a higher average temperature since they are so close to the equator.

38. C: The "X" indicates the process of evaporation on the water cycle diagram. The main water source for evaporation is the oceans as the oceans make up most of the water sources on our planet. Lakes, rivers, melted glaciers, and ponds contain water, but not nearly as much water as the oceans.

39. A: The immune system consists of the lymphatic system, spleen, tonsils, thymus, and bone marrow.

40. C: Leaves floating to the ground of the forest floor is an example of the law of gravity at work because gravity is pulling the leaves towards the Earth. A helicopter, a flying bird, and a floating balloon are all examples of objects overcoming gravity because they are moving away from the Earth, not being pulled toward the Earth.

41. D: With the warm temperature and cloudy conditions, rain could be expected. Since the temperature is 75 degrees Fahrenheit, it is well above freezing so snow and sleet would not be expected. There is no wind to blow the rain drops higher into the cooler atmosphere, so hail would not be expected.

42. C: The table won't move. The same amount of force is being applied by both men, but in opposite directions. This creates a balanced force which will not result in movement. Man A is pulling the table in his direction, but Man B is pulling with the same force in the opposite direction so the table will not move toward either man. When forces are equal, the object won't move, and a force would have to stop for it to fall to the ground.

43. D: The force of gravity pulls objects back toward the center of the Earth. The force of gravity is pulling the girl on the swing in the direction of the arrow, which is pointing back toward the Earth. Friction does not pull the girl in the direction of the arrow (A), and gravity pulls toward the center of the Earth (B). Gravity is always a pulling force, not a pushing one. The man pushing his daughter (C) would result in the girl moving forward, not in the direction of the arrow.

44. A: Choice A is an example of a learned behavior because someone had to teach the child to do this. It was not something he or she was born being able to do. Choice B and choice C are both examples of inherited traits because those are behaviors the fish and baby know how to do from birth. Choice D is an example of an inherited trait because this is something the skunk was born with.

45. D: In the ecosystem described, both coyotes and foxes are secondary consumers. Grass and corn are producers. Rabbits, crickets, squirrels, beetles, and grasshoppers are all primary consumers. Since foxes and coyotes consume different primary consumers, they are labeled as secondary consumers. Birds are also secondary consumers, but they are not a part of the options provided.

46. D: According to the description of the poison dart frog, the warm and rainy temperature of ecosystem T would be the best for it. Both the very cold climate found in ecosystem Q (A) and the very hot climate found in ecosystem R (B) would likely be too extreme for the frog. The plains, high summer temperatures, and lack of flowing water in ecosystem S (C) would not benefit the frog. The temperatures, streams, rivers, trees, and lush land found in ecosystem T make it a good habitat for the dart frog.

47. D: Step 6 of the experiment states the ingredients in the bottle are producing heat, which is a temperature change. A temperature change is a sign that a chemical reaction has happened. Adding dish soap, mixing the liquids, and combining mixtures do not, on their own, suggest a chemical reaction has occurred.

48. A: An acquired trait is a trait that a person or animal does not inherit but develops during their life. An inherited trait is passed down genetically. In this case, learning why the student's hair is red can let the student know if the trait is inherited. If her mother and/or father have red hair, it is likely an inherited trait. However, if the student dyed her hair, it would be acquired trait. Answer choice B is incorrect because, while having brown eyes is an inherited trait, her friend having brown eyes would not affect this trait. Answer choice C is incorrect because even if the student's grandmother has wrinkles, they are not hereditary. Older people acquire wrinkles because of age, skin damage, and lack of collagen, not because of genetics. Answer choice D is incorrect because even if the student's mother's ears are pierced, that does not mean that the student would also have her ears pierced. Having pierced ears is an acquired trait, not an inherited one.

49. D: Someone has taught the otters to roll over each time they hear a whistle. This requires training and is another example of learned behavior. The fish's fin size is an inherited trait of the species (A). Sea lions instinctively eat fish. This statement does not describe the sea lions going to a specific area or performing a trick for the fish. Simply eating the fish is an instinctive behavior (B). The height of the penguins is common for that species and an example of an inherited trait (C).

50. B, C: An instinct is a behavior that an animal performs from birth even if it has never seen another animal do the same behavior, while a learned behavior is one that an animal must learn to do from others or from experience. Answer choice B is correct because knowing if all cats bring mice back home would help the student understand if this behavior is instinctual. Instinctual behaviors are usually done by all members of a species, so if the answer is "no", this behavior is more likely to be a learned behavior. Answer choice C is correct because understanding if the cat meowed since it was a kitten would help the student understand if the behavior is learned or not. If the cat has not meowed since birth, then the cat is more likely to have learned this behavior by witnessing other cats meowing. Answer choice A is incorrect because understanding how high the cat's mother can jump does not help the student understand if jumping is a learned behavior. Instead, the student could ask, "Did the cat watch her mother jump before she attempted to jump?" Answer choice D is incorrect because understanding when the cat began to eat treats would not help the student understand if eating treats is instinctual or learned. While hunting for food may be an instinct, treats are not available in the wild. A better question would be, "Do all cats hunt for food?" or, "Do cats living alone hunt for food?"

51. C: An instinct is a behavior that an animal has the urge to do upon being born, whereas a learned behavior is something the animal must develop by observing others or through experience. If the crow can make tools from birth, that means this behavior is an instinct; however, if the crow does not know how to make tools until it sees other crows doing so, making tools is more likely a learned behavior. Answer choice A is incorrect because the time of year of nest-making has nothing to do with whether the behavior is learned or instinctual. Answer choice B is incorrect because it describes a physical characteristic of the crows instead of a behavior. Answer choice D is incorrect because knowing where crows of different colors live does not tell the student more about their behaviors. It would not help the student understand instinct or learned behavior, especially because the crows are the same species and should, therefore, have the same instincts.

52. B: Since the temperature is below freezing, the 5 inches of precipitation is expected to be snow, therefore building a snowman would be a common activity. The frozen precipitation would not result in puddles. The temperature would be too cold to go to the beach. It would not be a good day to fish with all the snow.

How to Overcome Test Anxiety

Just the thought of taking a test is enough to make most people a little nervous. A test is an important event that can have a long-term impact on your future, so it's important to take it seriously and it's natural to feel anxious about performing well. But just because anxiety is normal, that doesn't mean that it's helpful in test taking, or that you should simply accept it as part of your life. Anxiety can have a variety of effects. These effects can be mild, like making you feel slightly nervous, or severe, like blocking your ability to focus or remember even a simple detail.

If you experience test anxiety—whether severe or mild—it's important to know how to beat it. To discover this, first you need to understand what causes test anxiety.

Causes of Test Anxiety

While we often think of anxiety as an uncontrollable emotional state, it can actually be caused by simple, practical things. One of the most common causes of test anxiety is that a person does not feel adequately prepared for their test. This feeling can be the result of many different issues such as poor study habits or lack of organization, but the most common culprit is time management. Starting to study too late, failing to organize your study time to cover all of the material, or being distracted while you study will mean that you're not well prepared for the test. This may lead to cramming the night before, which will cause you to be physically and mentally exhausted for the test. Poor time management also contributes to feelings of stress, fear, and hopelessness as you realize you are not well prepared but don't know what to do about it.

Other times, test anxiety is not related to your preparation for the test but comes from unresolved fear. This may be a past failure on a test, or poor performance on tests in general. It may come from comparing yourself to others who seem to be performing better or from the stress of living up to expectations. Anxiety may be driven by fears of the future—how failure on this test would affect your educational and career goals. These fears are often completely irrational, but they can still negatively impact your test performance.

Elements of Test Anxiety

As mentioned earlier, test anxiety is considered to be an emotional state, but it has physical and mental components as well. Sometimes you may not even realize that you are suffering from test anxiety until you notice the physical symptoms. These can include trembling hands, rapid heartbeat, sweating, nausea, and tense muscles. Extreme anxiety may lead to fainting or vomiting. Obviously, any of these symptoms can have a negative impact on testing. It is important to recognize them as soon as they begin to occur so that you can address the problem before it damages your performance.

The mental components of test anxiety include trouble focusing and inability to remember learned information. During a test, your mind is on high alert, which can help you recall information and stay focused for an extended period of time. However, anxiety interferes with your mind's natural processes, causing you to blank out, even on the questions you know well. The strain of testing during anxiety makes it difficult to stay focused, especially on a test that may take several hours. Extreme anxiety can take a huge mental toll, making it difficult not only to recall test information but even to understand the test questions or pull your thoughts together.

Effects of Test Anxiety

Test anxiety is like a disease—if left untreated, it will get progressively worse. Anxiety leads to poor performance, and this reinforces the feelings of fear and failure, which in turn lead to poor performances on subsequent tests. It can grow from a mild nervousness to a crippling condition. If allowed to progress, test anxiety can have a big impact on your schooling, and consequently on your future.

Test anxiety can spread to other parts of your life. Anxiety on tests can become anxiety in any stressful situation, and blanking on a test can turn into panicking in a job situation. But fortunately, you don't have to let anxiety rule your testing and determine your grades. There are a number of relatively simple steps you can take to move past anxiety and function normally on a test and in the rest of life.

Physical Steps for Beating Test Anxiety

While test anxiety is a serious problem, the good news is that it can be overcome. It doesn't have to control your ability to think and remember information. While it may take time, you can begin taking steps today to beat anxiety.

Just as your first hint that you may be struggling with anxiety comes from the physical symptoms, the first step to treating it is also physical. Rest is crucial for having a clear, strong mind. If you are tired, it is much easier to give in to anxiety. But if you establish good sleep habits, your body and mind will be ready to perform optimally, without the strain of exhaustion. Additionally, sleeping well helps you to retain information better, so you're more likely to recall the answers when you see the test questions.

Getting good sleep means more than going to bed on time. It's important to allow your brain time to relax. Take study breaks from time to time so it doesn't get overworked, and don't study right before bed. Take time to rest your mind before trying to rest your body, or you may find it difficult to fall asleep.

Along with sleep, other aspects of physical health are important in preparing for a test. Good nutrition is vital for good brain function. Sugary foods and drinks may give a burst of energy but this burst is followed by a crash, both physically and emotionally. Instead, fuel your body with protein and vitamin-rich foods.

Also, drink plenty of water. Dehydration can lead to headaches and exhaustion, especially if your brain is already under stress from the rigors of the test. Particularly if your test is a long one, drink water during the breaks. And if possible, take an energy-boosting snack to eat between sections.

Along with sleep and diet, a third important part of physical health is exercise. Maintaining a steady workout schedule is helpful, but even taking 5-minute study breaks to walk can help get your blood pumping faster and clear your head. Exercise also releases endorphins, which contribute to a positive feeling and can help combat test anxiety.

When you nurture your physical health, you are also contributing to your mental health. If your body is healthy, your mind is much more likely to be healthy as well. So take time to rest, nourish your body with healthy food and water, and get moving as much as possible. Taking these physical steps will make you stronger and more able to take the mental steps necessary to overcome test anxiety.

Mental Steps for Beating Test Anxiety

Working on the mental side of test anxiety can be more challenging, but as with the physical side, there are clear steps you can take to overcome it. As mentioned earlier, test anxiety often stems from lack of preparation, so the obvious solution is to prepare for the test. Effective studying may be the most important weapon you have for beating test anxiety, but you can and should employ several other mental tools to combat fear.

First, boost your confidence by reminding yourself of past success—tests or projects that you aced. If you're putting as much effort into preparing for this test as you did for those, there's no reason you should expect to fail here. Work hard to prepare; then trust your preparation.

Second, surround yourself with encouraging people. It can be helpful to find a study group, but be sure that the people you're around will encourage a positive attitude. If you spend time with others who are anxious or cynical, this will only contribute to your own anxiety. Look for others who are motivated to study hard from a desire to succeed, not from a fear of failure.

Third, reward yourself. A test is physically and mentally tiring, even without anxiety, and it can be helpful to have something to look forward to. Plan an activity following the test, regardless of the outcome, such as going to a movie or getting ice cream.

When you are taking the test, if you find yourself beginning to feel anxious, remind yourself that you know the material. Visualize successfully completing the test. Then take a few deep, relaxing breaths and return to it. Work through the questions carefully but with confidence, knowing that you are capable of succeeding.

Developing a healthy mental approach to test taking will also aid in other areas of life. Test anxiety affects more than just the actual test—it can be damaging to your mental health and even contribute to depression. It's important to beat test anxiety before it becomes a problem for more than testing.

Study Strategy

Being prepared for the test is necessary to combat anxiety, but what does being prepared look like? You may study for hours on end and still not feel prepared. What you need is a strategy for test prep. The next few pages outline our recommended steps to help you plan out and conquer the challenge of preparation.

Step 1: Scope Out the Test

Learn everything you can about the format (multiple choice, essay, etc.) and what will be on the test. Gather any study materials, course outlines, or sample exams that may be available. Not only will this help you to prepare, but knowing what to expect can help to alleviate test anxiety.

Step 2: Map Out the Material

Look through the textbook or study guide and make note of how many chapters or sections it has. Then divide these over the time you have. For example, if a book has 15 chapters and you have five days to study, you need to cover three chapters each day. Even better, if you have the time, leave an extra day at the end for overall review after you have gone through the material in depth.

If time is limited, you may need to prioritize the material. Look through it and make note of which sections you think you already have a good grasp on, and which need review. While you are studying, skim quickly through the familiar sections and take more time on the challenging parts.

Write out your plan so you don't get lost as you go. Having a written plan also helps you feel more in control of the study, so anxiety is less likely to arise from feeling overwhelmed at the amount to cover.

Step 3: Gather Your Tools

Decide what study method works best for you. Do you prefer to highlight in the book as you study and then go back over the highlighted portions? Or do you type out notes of the important information? Or is it helpful to make flashcards that you can carry with you? Assemble the pens, index cards, highlighters, post-it notes, and any other materials you may need so you won't be distracted by getting up to find things while you study.

If you're having a hard time retaining the information or organizing your notes, experiment with different methods. For example, try color-coding by subject with colored pens, highlighters, or post-it notes. If you learn better by hearing, try recording yourself reading your notes so you can listen while in the car, working out, or simply sitting at your desk. Ask a friend to quiz you from your flashcards, or try teaching someone the material to solidify it in your mind.

Step 4: Create Your Environment

It's important to avoid distractions while you study. This includes both the obvious distractions like visitors and the subtle distractions like an uncomfortable chair (or a too-comfortable couch that makes you want to fall asleep). Set up the best study environment possible: good lighting and a comfortable work area. If background music helps you focus, you may want to turn it on, but otherwise keep the room quiet. If you are using a computer to take notes, be sure you don't have any other windows open, especially applications like social media, games, or anything else that could distract you. Silence your phone and turn off notifications. Be sure to keep water close by so you stay hydrated while you study (but avoid unhealthy drinks and snacks).

Also, take into account the best time of day to study. Are you freshest first thing in the morning? Try to set aside some time then to work through the material. Is your mind clearer in the afternoon or evening? Schedule your study session then. Another method is to study at the same time of day that you will take the test, so that your brain gets used to working on the material at that time and will be ready to focus at test time.

Step 5: Study!

Once you have done all the study preparation, it's time to settle into the actual studying. Sit down, take a few moments to settle your mind so you can focus, and begin to follow your study plan. Don't give in to distractions or let yourself procrastinate. This is your time to prepare so you'll be ready to fearlessly approach the test. Make the most of the time and stay focused.

Of course, you don't want to burn out. If you study too long you may find that you're not retaining the information very well. Take regular study breaks. For example, taking five minutes out of every hour to walk briskly, breathing deeply and swinging your arms, can help your mind stay fresh.

As you get to the end of each chapter or section, it's a good idea to do a quick review. Remind yourself of what you learned and work on any difficult parts. When you feel that you've mastered the material, move on to the next part. At the end of your study session, briefly skim through your notes again.

But while review is helpful, cramming last minute is NOT. If at all possible, work ahead so that you won't need to fit all your study into the last day. Cramming overloads your brain with more information than it can process and retain, and your tired mind may struggle to recall even previously learned information when it is overwhelmed with last-minute study. Also, the urgent nature of cramming and the stress placed on your brain contribute to anxiety. You'll be more likely to go to the test feeling unprepared and having trouble thinking clearly.

So don't cram, and don't stay up late before the test, even just to review your notes at a leisurely pace. Your brain needs rest more than it needs to go over the information again. In fact, plan to finish your studies by noon or early afternoon the day before the test. Give your brain the rest of the day to relax or focus on other things, and get a good night's sleep. Then you will be fresh for the test and better able to recall what you've studied.

Step 6: Take a Practice Test

Many courses offer sample tests, either online or in the study materials. This is an excellent resource to check whether you have mastered the material, as well as to prepare for the test format and environment.

Check the test format ahead of time: the number of questions, the type (multiple choice, free response, etc.), and the time limit. Then create a plan for working through them. For example, if you have 30 minutes to take a 60-question test, your limit is 30 seconds per question. Spend less time on the questions you know well so that you can take more time on the difficult ones.

If you have time to take several practice tests, take the first one open book, with no time limit. Work through the questions at your own pace and make sure you fully understand them. Gradually work up to taking a test under test conditions: sit at a desk with all study materials put away and set a timer. Pace yourself to make sure you finish the test with time to spare and go back to check your answers if you have time.

After each test, check your answers. On the questions you missed, be sure you understand why you missed them. Did you misread the question (tests can use tricky wording)? Did you forget the information? Or was it something you hadn't learned? Go back and study any shaky areas that the practice tests reveal.

Taking these tests not only helps with your grade, but also aids in combating test anxiety. If you're already used to the test conditions, you're less likely to worry about it, and working through tests until you're scoring well gives you a confidence boost. Go through the practice tests until you feel comfortable, and then you can go into the test knowing that you're ready for it.

Test Tips

On test day, you should be confident, knowing that you've prepared well and are ready to answer the questions. But aside from preparation, there are several test day strategies you can employ to maximize your performance.

First, as stated before, get a good night's sleep the night before the test (and for several nights before that, if possible). Go into the test with a fresh, alert mind rather than staying up late to study.

Try not to change too much about your normal routine on the day of the test. It's important to eat a nutritious breakfast, but if you normally don't eat breakfast at all, consider eating just a protein bar. If you're a coffee drinker, go ahead and have your normal coffee. Just make sure you time it so that the caffeine doesn't wear off right in the middle of your test. Avoid sugary beverages, and drink enough water to stay hydrated but not so much that you need a restroom break 10 minutes into the test. If your test isn't first thing in the morning, consider going for a walk or doing a light workout before the test to get your blood flowing.

Allow yourself enough time to get ready, and leave for the test with plenty of time to spare so you won't have the anxiety of scrambling to arrive in time. Another reason to be early is to select a good seat. It's helpful to sit away from doors and windows, which can be distracting. Find a good seat, get out your supplies, and settle your mind before the test begins.

When the test begins, start by going over the instructions carefully, even if you already know what to expect. Make sure you avoid any careless mistakes by following the directions.

Then begin working through the questions, pacing yourself as you've practiced. If you're not sure on an answer, don't spend too much time on it, and don't let it shake your confidence. Either skip it and come back later, or eliminate as many wrong answers as possible and guess among the remaining ones. Don't dwell on these questions as you continue—put them out of your mind and focus on what lies ahead.

Be sure to read all of the answer choices, even if you're sure the first one is the right answer. Sometimes you'll find a better one if you keep reading. But don't second-guess yourself if you do immediately know the answer. Your gut instinct is usually right. Don't let test anxiety rob you of the information you know.

If you have time at the end of the test (and if the test format allows), go back and review your answers. Be cautious about changing any, since your first instinct tends to be correct, but make sure you didn't misread any of the questions or accidentally mark the wrong answer choice. Look over any you skipped and make an educated guess.

At the end, leave the test feeling confident. You've done your best, so don't waste time worrying about your performance or wishing you could change anything. Instead, celebrate the successful completion of this test. And finally, use this test to learn how to deal with anxiety even better next time.

Review Video: Test Anxiety
Visit mometrix.com/academy and enter code: 100340

Important Qualification

Not all anxiety is created equal. If your test anxiety is causing major issues in your life beyond the classroom or testing center, or if you are experiencing troubling physical symptoms related to your anxiety, it may be a sign of a serious physiological or psychological condition. If this sounds like your situation, we strongly encourage you to seek professional help.

Online Resources

Due to our efforts to try to keep this book to a manageable length, we've created a link that will give you access to all of your online resources:

mometrix.com/resources719/ssncg5sci

It's Your Moment, Let's Celebrate It!

Share your story @mometrixtestpreparation